Inquiries About Shi'a Islam

Second Edition

Imam Sayed Moustafa al-Qazwini

The Islamic Educational Center
of Orange County–California

Published by
The Islamic Educational Center of Orange County
3194-B Airport Loop Drive
Costa Mesa, California, 92626, U.S.A.
Telephone: (714) 432- 6
Fax: (714) 432- 7
http://www.iecoc.org
info@iecoc.org

Library of Congress Catalog Number: 99- 75772
British Library Cataloguing in Publication Data

ISBN: 1- 794 2-67-X
2nd Edition-2 5

Cover Design and Typesetting
by Islamic Publishing House [www.iph.ca]

Printed in Canada by Webcom Limited
www.webcomlink.com

بِسْمِ ٱللَّهِ ٱلرَّحْمَٰنِ ٱلرَّحِيمِ ۝

ٱلْحَمْدُ لِلَّهِ رَبِّ ٱلْعَٰلَمِينَ ۝ ٱلرَّحْمَٰنِ ٱلرَّحِيمِ ۝ مَٰلِكِ

يَوْمِ ٱلدِّينِ ۝ إِيَّاكَ نَعْبُدُ وَإِيَّاكَ نَسْتَعِينُ ۝

ٱهْدِنَا ٱلصِّرَٰطَ ٱلْمُسْتَقِيمَ ۝ صِرَٰطَ ٱلَّذِينَ أَنْعَمْتَ عَلَيْهِمْ

غَيْرِ ٱلْمَغْضُوبِ عَلَيْهِمْ وَلَا ٱلضَّآلِّينَ ۝

In the Name of Allah, the Infinitely Compassionate, the Most Merciful

All praise belongs to Allah, the Lord of Mankind.
The Most Gracious, the Most Merciful.
Master of the Day of Recompense.
You alone do we worship,
and You alone do we ask for help.
Guide us to the straight path,
the path of those upon whom
You have bestowed Your grace,
not of those with whom You are angered,
nor of those who have gone astray.[1]

---

[1] Noble Quran, Surah (ch.) 1

I offer this humble work in the service of the Almighty Allah—the Creator, Lord, Cherisher, and Sustainer of the Heavens and Earth—and I dedicate it to His beloved servant and messenger, Prophet Muhammad (*pbuh&hf*), his righteous family, and his pious companions.

It is customary in Islam that when the name of Allah, Prophet Muhammad, the other Prophets, or Imams (descendants and successors of Prophet Muhammad) are enunciated, the following phrases are mentioned:

Allah—*"Glorified and Exalted"*
(Subhanna wa-tallah)
Written abbreviation—*SWT*

Prophet Muhammad—*"Peace be upon him and his family"*
Written abbreviation—*pbuh&hf*

After the names of the other Prophets, Imams from the family of Prophet Muhammad, and his daughter—*"Peace be upon him/her"*
Written abbreviation—*pbuh.*

With great respect, admiration, acknowledgment, and praise, I have omitted the mentioned phrases for the sake of continuity.

Table of Contents

بِسْمِ ٱللَّهِ ٱلرَّحْمَٰنِ ٱلرَّحِيمِ

ٱلَّذِينَ يَسْتَمِعُونَ ٱلْقَوْلَ فَيَتَّبِعُونَ أَحْسَنَهُۥ أُوْلَٰئِكَ ٱلَّذِينَ هَدَىٰهُمُ ٱللَّهُ وَأُوْلَٰئِكَ هُمْ أُوْلُواْ ٱلْأَلْبَٰبِ ۝

Introduction

Bismillahir Rahmanir Rahim
Those who listen to the Word and follow the best of it:
those are the ones whom Allah has guided, and
those are the ones with understanding.[1]

The Shi'a and Sunni schools of thought form the two wings of the Islamic nation that allow it to fly and carry out its lofty objectives. A great Muslim scholar once said, "Those who attempt to cause division between the Shi'a and Sunni are neither Shi'a nor Sunni." Written under this premise, the book in hand should clarify some common questions and inquiries about the philosophy and practice of Shi'a Islam. The Shi'a and Sunni schools of thought differ primarily in jurisprudence and have far more similarities than differences. Every school of thought in Islam must be respected because they all can lead people to salvation.

Due to the lack of clear information, the Shi'a *Imamiyyah* school of thought has remained a mystery to many Muslims. Numerous Muslims are relieved to discover the truth about Shi'a Islam from reliable sources. Nevertheless, the enemies of Islam have found that the best way to slander Islam and disturb the peace within the Muslim nation is to encourage division and sectarianism. Thus, a myriad of negative and false rumors with no basis in the authentic books of the Shi'a school of thought have been spread. These

---

[1] *Noble Quran,* 39:18

rumors have two sources: animosity towards Islam on the part of those who invent them, and ignorance on the part of those who believe and propagate them.

This book is a call to unite the Muslims since true unity stems from an understanding of each other's philosophies, not from keeping them secret. While the majority of Shi'a scholars and even average individuals keep many books belonging to other schools of thought in their libraries, few other Muslims take the time to read the original sources of Shi'a philosophy. I have endeavored in this book to present the most controversial issues that distinguish Shi'a Islam in a simple manner understandable by all people, particularly our youth generation in the Western countries. To make this book accessible to all readers regardless of their school of thought, I have relied mainly on the Noble Quran and traditions of the Prophet Muhammad (PBUH&HF) as reported in the books of narration (hadith).

I have endeavored to be as accurate and scientific as possible in presenting what has been recorded in the commonly accepted Islamic sources. I share the aspiration of most Muslims to see the Muslim nation heed to the call of the Noble Quran, "Truly your nation is one nation, and I am your Lord. Therefore, worship Me."[2]

Another aim is to build a strong, cohesive, and cooperative Muslim community around the globe, and for this nation to be respected it must be united. Muslims must understand and accept each other's positions and principles. The best way to disperse the misunderstandings and misconceptions between the schools of thought is through constructive, sincere, and objective dialogue. If the Noble Quran invites the adherents of the three monotheistic religions (Judaism, Christianity, and Islam) to share dialogue in a civilized manner[3] then certainly the schools of Islamic thought should also come together to discuss their differences based on the

---

[2] *Noble Quran*, 21:92
[3] *Noble Quran*, 3:64

Noble Quran and the authentic traditions of the Prophet Muhammad (PBUH&HF). While none can deny that the schools of thought have juristic (*fiqh*) differences, these differences should not prevent adherents to these schools from acknowledging and respecting each other's opinions, for the leaders of these schools of thought acquired their knowledge from one source—the Prophet and ultimately Almighty Allah.

Almighty Allah created human beings with both an inner messenger and an outer messenger. Both, the inner messenger, which is the brain or the reasoning faculty, and the outer messenger, which is the divine revelation, invite a person to exercise his or her own intellectual abilities to search for the truth, and not to take their customs, traditions, or family behavior as sacred beliefs. This call is directed to the followers of all the branches of Islam. All Muslims must research and study their history and not be bound by the customs and traditions of their ancestors which may not rest on solid ground, for the Noble Quran condemns the blind following of ancestors as follows:

> And when it is said to them, 'Come to what Allah has revealed and to the Messenger.' They say, 'enough for us is that which we found our fathers following,' even though their fathers had no knowledge whatsoever and no guidance.[4]

> When it is said to them, 'Follow what Allah has sent down.' They say, 'Nay! We shall follow what we found our fathers following.' Would they do that even though their fathers did not understand anything, nor were they guided?[5]

I ask all who read this book to read it objectively, with open-mindedness and without sectarian biases, and I welcome any suggestions, criticisms, or inquiries.

---

[4] *Noble Quran*, 5:104
[5] *Noble Quran*, 2:170

We ask Allah for guidance and enlightenment in our search for the truth. May Allah open our hearts and minds to it, and may He guide and extend His mercy upon us, for He is the one who grants all things. "Our Lord! Let not our hearts deviate from the truth after You have guided us, and grant us mercy from You; truly, You are the Bestower."[6]

We ask Allah for His mercy, grace, and blessings in this endeavor, and I ask the readers for their prayers that we all continue to be humble servants of the religion of Allah on the Earth.

Sayed Moustafa al-Qazwini
August 13, 1999
Orange County, California

---

[6] *Noble Quran,* 3:8

Introduction to Second Edition

Since the first edition of *Inquiries about Shia Islam* was published in the summer of 1999, four-thousand English copies have been distributed and sold to Muslims and non-Muslims in the United States of America and abroad. The book was also published in various languages. The need still exists for a better understanding about the traditions and followers of the Ahlul Bayt, and thus a revised second edition of the book was made. I would like to take this opportunity to thank Sister Fatma Saleh for her generous contributions in editing and revising this edition. Special thanks are also due to the Khaki family of Seattle, Washington for making this book come to print. May Allah, the most Merciful, the most Compassionate reward all those who work sincerely to serve His cause.

Sayed Moustafa al-Qazwini
October 17, 2005
Ramadan 13, 1426
Orange County, California

Who are the Shi'a?

The fifth imam of the school of the Ahlul Bayt, Imam Muhammad al-Baqir once told his student by the name of Jabir, "Is it enough for a person to embellish himself as our Shi'a (follower) by professing love for us, the Ahlul Bayt? Nay! By Allah, a person is not our follower unless he fears Allah and obeys Him. Our followers are only recognized, O Jabir, by their humility, submission, honesty, abundant praise of Allah, fasting, prayers, goodness to their parents, attention to the poor, needy, debtors, and orphans living nearby, speaking of the truth, recitation of the Quran, holding back their tongues except for good words, and trustworthiness towards one's relatives in all affairs."[1]

"Shi'a" means *a group of followers* and it occurs in the Quran many times in reference to the followers of the previous prophets, such as Prophet Ibrahim (Abraham) and Prophet Musa (Moses).[2] Shi'a today refers to the followers of a particular school of Islamic thought, which is based on the teachings of the Prophet and his family, and sometimes it is referred to as the "school of Ahlul Bayt" (the family of the Prophet). While no schools of thought existed at the time of the Prophet Muhammad, he still used to refer to a certain group of people as the "Shi'a of Ali."

Some narrations in which the Prophet Muhammad used the term "Shi'a of Ali" are as follows:

> The parable of Ali is like a tree, in which I am the root, Ali is the branch, Hassan and Husayn are the fruits, and the Shi'a are the leaves.[3] (Ibn Hajar)

---

[1] *al-Kulayni*, al-Kafi, Vol. 2, 74

[2] *Noble Quran*, 28.15

[3] Ibn Hajar, *Lisan al-Mizan*, Vol. 2, 354

> We were gathering around the Prophet when Ali ibn Abi Talib came. He said, 'Verily, my brother has come to you,' and he placed his hand on the Ka'bah and said, 'By the One Who holds my soul in His hand, this man and his Shi'a will indeed be the successful ones on the Day of Judgment.'[4] (Narrated by Jabir ibn 'Abdillah al-Ansari)

> The Prophet of Allah was with me when his daughter Lady Fatima came to greet him with her husband Ali. The Prophet of Allah raised his head and said, 'Be happy Ali; you and your Shi'a will be in Paradise.'[5] (Narrated by Um Salamah, the wife of the Prophet Muhammad)

> You and your Shi'a will be in Paradise.[6]

As these narrations show, the Prophet Muhammad himself was in fact, the first person to use the term "Shi'a," and what's more is that he always used the term in reference to Imam Ali. After the Prophet passed away those who were loyal to Imam Ali were also known as the Shi'a. During the second century Hijrah (i.e., two centuries after the migration of the Prophet Muhammad from the city of Makkah to the city of Madina—the event which marks the beginning of the Islamic calendar), the Abbasid caliphs officially patronized the four Sunni schools of thought which were popularized by the enthusiasm of some of their leaders. As for the Shi'a, after the assassination of Imam Ali, they followed the leadership of his son Hassan, and after him his brother Husayn, and the subsequent nine imams who were the descendants of Husayn. They followed them on the firm basis of evidence in the Noble Quran and the tradition of Prophet Muhammad who explicitly repeated on many occasions that he [the Prophet] would be

---

[4] *Tawzih al-Dala'il fiTashih al-Fada'il*, 505

[5] Ibid., 507

[6] Ibn Asakir, *"The History of the City of Damascus"* Section: Biography of Imam Ali

followed by twelve imams and that they would all be from the tribe of Quraysh.[7]

Therefore, Shi'ism can be termed as the following of the Noble Quran and the tradition of Prophet Muhammad as conveyed by his family, whom he appointed (i.e., the Ahlul Bayt). After the Prophet Muhammad, the Shi'a followed the twelve divinely ordained imams as successors of the Prophet Muhammad, as will be seen in the subsequent sections.

---

[7] *Sahih al-Bukhari; Sahih Muslim,* Vol. 2, 191; *Sahih al-Tirmidhi,* Vol. 2, 45; *Musnad* Ahmad ibn Hanbal, Vol. 5, 106; *Sunan* Abu Dawud, Vol. 2, 207

The Five Schools of Islamic Thought

Schools of Islamic thought (*madhahib*) are the paths people follow to the Noble Quran and Prophet Muhammad. Obviously, these schools of thought were founded considerably after the death of the Prophet; in fact, they never took shape until the time of the Umayyid Caliphate. The common phrase *ahl al-sunnah wal-jama'ah*, for example, became prevalent during the third century of the Hijrah. By the year 250H, the four Sunni schools of thought were being popularized and patronized during the Abbasid Caliphate. The Shi'a school of thought on the other hand, continued its growth and progress after Imam Ali through his descendants who were connected to each other through a chain of narration and knowledge. Prophet Muhammad and the designated imams in the Shi'a school of thought were shielded by Allah from any sin, religious error, or forgetfulness.

Today, the five schools of Islamic thought accepted by all Muslims are the Ja'fari, comprising 23% of the Muslims; the Hanafi, comprising 31% of the Muslims; the Maliki, comprising 25% of the Muslims; the Shafi'i, comprising 16% of the Muslims; and the Hanbali, comprising 4% of the Muslims. The remaining small percentage follow other minority schools, such as the Zaydi and the Isma'ili.[1]

Ja'fari

The Ja'fari school of thought was headed by Imam Ja'far ibn Muhammad al-Sadiq who lived from 83H to 148H. He was born in and died in the holy city of Madina, and he is the sixth Imam of the twelve designated imams of the school of Ahlul Bayt. Although the *fiqh* (Islamic Jurisprudence) was developed by the Prophet

---

[1] *"Bulletin of Affiliation"* Al-Madhhab Schools of Thought Statistic - Dec. 1998, Vol. 17-4. 5

Muhammad and his successors (i.e., the imams), the fiqh, as taught by the Shi'a, did not have the opportunity to be presented to the masses of people because of the political predicament that the Ahlul Bayt suffered under the rulers for many centuries. The imams refused to acknowledge the legitimacy of the Umayyad and Abbasid caliphs, and their governments; and thus they and their followers were exposed to tremendous harassment and persecution at the hands of the unjust caliphs. Once the Umayyad government became weak, Imam Ja'far ibn Muhammad al-Sadiq found a golden opportunity to formulate and spread the tradition of the Prophet Muhammad and his family. At one time, four thousand scholars, commentators of the Quran, historians, and philosophers attended his classes in the holy city of Madina. Therefore, he was able to pass down the authentic teachings of the Noble Quran and the Prophet Muhammad and crystallize them in what came to be known as *al-Fiqh al-Ja'fari*, the Ja'fari Jurisprudence. His teachings were collected in 400 *usul* (foundations) which were written by his students and encompass hadith, Islamic philosophy, theology, commentary of the Quran, literature, and ethics.

After a period of time, three distinguished scholars categorized these 400 usul in four books which are the main sources of hadith for the Shi'a school of thought. They are: *Usul al-Kafi* by al-Kulayni (d.329H), *Man La Yahduruh al-Faqih* by al-Saduq (d.381H), and *al-Tahdib* and *al-Istibsar* by al-Tusi (d.460H). These three scholars were known as the "three Muhammads" since their first names were all Muhammad. While these four books are the main sources of hadith for the Shi'a, their authors still did not label their books as "*sahih*" (authentic). Although they did their best to gather only authentic traditions, but if a particular tradition contradicted the Noble Quran then it was not accepted as legal and valid. Hadith, according to the Ja'fari school of thought, are accepted only if the Noble Quran verifies them, since the Noble Quran is the only undoubtable source of guidance.

Hanafi

The Hanafi school of thought was headed by Imam al-Nu'man ibn Thabit (Abu Hanifa) who lived from 80H to 150H. Imam Abu Hanifa was born to a non-Arab father, was raised in Kufa, and died in Baghdad. This school of thought prevailed during the time of the Abbasid Empire when a student of Imam Abu Hanifa, Abu Yusuf al-Qadi became the head of the judiciary department and the highest judge, and thus he spread this *madhhab* (school of thought), in particular, during the caliphates of al-Mahdi, al-Hadi, and al-Rashid. No other man was as close to the Abbasid caliph, Harun al-Rashid as was Abu Yusuf al-Qadi, but the Abbasid caliph, al-Mansur also worked hard to support and consolidate Imam Abu Hanifa's school of thought and to spread his madhhab in the face of the growing popularity of Imam Ja'far al-Sadiq. Imam Abu Hanifa studied under the instruction of Imam Ja'far al-Sadiq for two years,[2] and said in regards to him, "I have not seen anyone more knowledgeable than Ja'far ibn Muhammad, and indeed, he is the most knowledgeable one in the nation."[3]

Maliki

The Maliki school of thought was headed by Imam Malik ibn Anas al-Asbahi who lived from 93H to 179H. He was born in the holy city of Madina, and his fame spread throughout Hijaz. On the account of his disagreement with Imam Abu Hanifa, Imam Malik became the leader of the school of tradition (*hadith*), while Imam Abu Hanifa was the leader of the school of opinion (*ra'i*). Yet, most Muslim governments were supportive of Imam Abu Hanifa.

Imam Malik joined the *'Alawiyiin*, the descendants of Imam Ali, and received his knowledge from Imam Ja'far al-Sadiq, but thereafter, inconsistencies marked his life. At one point he was oppressed and having earned the anger of the government, he was dragged through the streets by his clothes and lashed. In 148H, his

---

[2] Kalili, *Min Amali al-Imam al-Sadiq*, Vol. 4, 157
[3] *Tadhkirat al-Hiffadh*, Vol. 1, 166; *Asna al-Matalib*, 55

fortunes reversed and he regained his popularity and dominance. The Abbasids tried to set him up as a popular reference for the nation in giving verdicts and injunctions. The Abbasid caliph al-Mansur asked him to write *al-Muwatta'*, his book of fiqh, which contains the principles of the Maliki school of thought. Furthermore, during the hajj season, the official announcer of the government proclaimed that no one had the authority to give *fatawas* (religious decisions) except for Imam Malik. The Abbasid caliph Harun al-Rashid sat on the floor to listen to him, and the caliphate in general exalted him to the point where they said that no book on earth, except the Noble Quran, was more authentic than that of Imam Malik's. Ibn Hazm al-Andalusi says that two schools of thought were spread due to the government and the sultan: the school of Imam Abu Hanifa, since Abu Yusuf al-Qadi only appointed Hanafi judges; and the school of Imam Malik ibn Anas, for a student of Imam Malik, Yahya ibn Yahya was so respected in the caliph's palace that no judge was ever appointed in Andalus, Spain without his consultation and advice.

Shafi'i

The Shafi'i school of thought was headed by Imam Muhammad ibn Idris al-Shafi'i who lived from 150H to 198H. Imam Shafi'i was born in Hijaz and his school of thought emerged in Egypt. At the time of the Fatimid Dynasty, the Egyptians were mainly followers of Ahlul Bayt, and the teachings of Ahlul Bayt were being taught in al-Azhar University. At a later time, Salah al-Din al-Ayyubi came and waged an extensive war against the school of Ahlul Bayt by banning the teaching of their madhhab (school of thought) in al-Azhar and resurrecting the other madhahib, including that of Imam Shafi'i, who was killed in Egypt in 198H.

Hanbali

The Hanbali school of thought was headed by Imam Ahmad ibn Hanbal who lived from 164H to 241H. He was born and died in Baghdad. He only gained popularity in Najd (a region of the Arabian Peninsula) due to the ideas of Muhammad ibn 'Abd al-Wahhab, the founder of Wahabism. The Hanbali madhhab spread in Najd primarily due to the teachings of Ahmad ibn 'Abd al-Halim al-Dimishqi ibn Taymiyyah (661H–728H) and his student ibn al-Qayyim al-Jawziyya.

A close study of the history of the madhahibs and a search into the reasons for their birth, existence, and spread, reveals that the various governments were the main factor in the birth and spread of these schools. Governmental aid took physical and financial forms by establishing schools, sponsoring books of *fiqh* (law), adopting and sponsoring official madhahib, and giving freedom to the founders and scholars of some of the "official" madhahib. This trend has occurred in almost every religion worldwide; for example, one might compare this trend in Islam to the birth of the Anglican Church in 1534AD by the English king, Henry VIII who made it the official religious tradition of the state, thus giving it 55 million followers.

History tells that the school of Ahlul Bayt suffered extreme oppression, tyranny, and discrimination at the hands of the Umayyad and 'Abbasid caliphs. But in spite of oppression, by the divine will of Allah, the school of the Ahlul Bayt reached a climax during the caliphate of al-Ma'mun, and Shi'ism reached so far into the governmental dignitaries that al-Ma'mun himself was forced to show deep sympathy towards the *'Alawiyiin*, the descendants of Imam Ali, and to show an inclination towards Shi'ism, to the point that he invited Imam Ali ibn Musa al-Rida, the eighth Imam of the Ahlul Bayt to be his successor—a position which Imam al-Rida declined.

Imamah

The major distinction between the school of Ahlul Bayt and the other Islamic schools of thought revolves around the issue of *Imamah*, or the early succession to Prophet Muhammad. The school of Ahlul Bayt maintains that the office of the imamah is a divine office - meaning, the *imam* or *khalifah* (leadership) has to be appointed and given directly by Allah, for this office holds the same significance as that of prophethood. People are thus commanded by Allah to follow specific successors (*imams*) after the demise of the Prophet.

Other schools of thought say that the imamah is determined by *shura* (election) and that this method was used to determine the successor of the Prophet Muhammad. However, the Shi'a school of thought considers that the concept of shura was never fully enacted after the death of the Prophet because ibn Qutaybah asserts that the first caliph was nominated mainly by two people;[1] Ibn Kathir says that he had confined the candidacy for the khilafah to 'Umar ibn al-Khattab and Abu 'Ubaydah ibn al-Jarrah, both of whom declined and nominated him, a nomination that was seconded by Ma'adh, 'Usayd, Bashir, and Zayd ibn Thabit.[2] Tabari narrates that the Ansar refused to submit to his allegiance in al-Saqifah (the place where the matter of immediate succession to the Prophet was discussed) and declared that they would only pay allegiance to Ali (because he was the one appointed by the Prophet to be his successor).[3] The first caliph has been recorded to have said in his inaugural ceremony, "O people! I was appointed over you, but I am not the best one among you."[4] Historian ibn Abi al-Hadid al-Mu'tazili records that the second

---

[1] Ibn Qutaybah, *al-Imamah wal-Siyasah*, Vol. 1, 6,
[2] Ibn Kathir, *al-Sira al-Nabawiyyah*, Vol. 2, 494
[3] al-Tabari *Tarikh*, Vol. 2, 443
[4] al-Suyuti, *Tarikh al-Khulafa'*, 69

caliph admitted his role in orchestrating the meeting at al-Saqifah when he later declared that paying allegiance to the first caliph had been a mistake (*faltah*) but that Allah had averted the disaster of it from the Muslims.[5] The concept of shura however was not implemented during the second caliph's ascension to the caliphate since the first caliph appointed him before his death. It was not even enacted during the ascension of the third caliph to power, since he was also selected nominally by five people, but in essence by one— namely, the second caliph, who also appointed two governors to remain in power after his death namely: Sa'd ibn Abi Waqqass and Abu Musa al-Ash'ari.[6]

Quranic Evidence for the Divine Ordination of the Imam

Numerous verses in the Noble Quran refer to the fact that throughout history Allah alone has the right to ordain an *imam* (leader) or *khalifah* for mankind – some of them are as follows:

> And remember when your Lord said to the angels, 'Verily, I am going to place [for mankind] a successor (khalifah) on the earth.'[7]

> O David! Verily We have placed you as a successor (khalifah) on the earth, so judge between men with truth and justice, and follow not your desires, for they will mislead you from the path of Allah.[8]

> And remember when the Lord of Abraham tried him with certain commands which he fulfilled. Allah said to him, 'Verily I am going to make you a leader (imam) for mankind.' Abraham said, 'And

---

[5] Ibn Abi al-Hadid al-Mu'tazili, *Sharh Nahj al-Balaghah*, Vol. 2, 29
[6] Ibid., Vol. 9, 50
[7] *Noble Quran*, 2:30
[8] *Noble Quran*, 38:26

(what about) my offspring?' Allah said, 'My providence (does not) includes the wrongdoers.'[9]

And We made from among them leaders (imams), giving guidance under Our command, when they were patient and believed with certainty in Our proofs and evidence.[10]

These verses clarify that not just anyone is entitled to assume the office of leadership or the *imamah* and one who qualifies for this is the one who Allah examines and he fulfills Allah's test. In particular, the Noble Quran in the above verse of 2:124 stresses very clearly that the wrongdoers (*dhalimeen*) are forbidden from assuming the leadership of the believers. Yet, does Islamic history show this command to have been carried out? How many caliphs and sultans during the Umayyad and Abbasid periods were corrupt and did not practice Islam properly, yet they were leaders of the Muslim nation?

Succession—khilafah or imamah—is appointed solely by Allah whenever it is mentioned in the Noble Quran. In the school of Ahlul Bayt, the khilafah refers not only to temporal power and political authority over the people but more importantly, it indicates the authority to do so. This authority must be from Allah since Allah attributes governing and judgment to Himself.

Seven Categories of Verses of Allah's Government in the Quran

(1) The Verses of Kingdom:

Say, 'O Allah! Possessor of the Kingdom! You give the Kingdom to whom You will, and You take the Kingdom from whom You will.'[11]

---

[9] *Noble Quran,* 2:124
[10] *Noble Quran,* 32:24
[11] *Noble Quran,* 3:26

Say, 'I seek refuge with Allah, the Lord of Mankind, the King of Mankind, the God of Mankind....'[12]

To Allah belongs the domain of the heavens and the earth and all that is between them, and to Him will all return.[13]

(2) The Verses of Government:

The decision (*hukm*) is only for Allah. He declares the truth, and He is the best of judges.[14]

Surely, His is the judgment, and He is the swiftest in taking account.[15]

And in whatsoever you differ, the decision thereof is with Allah. He is the ruling judge.[16]

(3) The Verses of Command:

Say, 'Indeed, the command (*'amr*) belongs entirely to Allah.'[17]

Surely, His is the creation and the command. Blessed be Allah, the Lord of Mankind.[18]

But the decision of all things is certainly with Allah.[19]

It is not for a believer, man or woman, when Allah and His Messenger have decreed a matter that they should have any opinion in their decision. And

---

[12] *Noble Quran,* 114:1-3
[13] *Noble Quran,* 5:18
[14] *Noble Quran,* 6:57
[15] *Noble Quran,* 6:62
[16] *Noble Quran,* 42:10
[17] *Noble Quran,* 3:154
[18] *Noble Quran,* 7:54
[19] *Noble Quran,* 13:31

whoever disobeys Allah and His Messenger, he has indeed strayed in plain error.[20]

(4) The Verses of Guardianship:

Verily, your guardian (*wali*) is Allah, His Messenger, and the believers—those who perform the prayers and give *zakat* (alms) while bowing down (*ruku*).[21]

Commentators unanimously agree that this particular verse refers to Imam Ali ibn Abi Talib who gave his ring to a beggar while in the state of bowing (*ruku*) in the course of his prayer.

The only saying of the faithful believers, when they are called to Allah and His Messenger to judge between them, is that they say, 'We hear and we obey,' and such are the prosperous ones.[22]

We sent no messenger but to be obeyed by Allah's leave.[23]

By your Lord, they can have no faith until they make you (Prophet Muhammad) a judge in all disputes between them and find in themselves no resistance against your decision and accept it with full submission.[24]

(5) The Verses of Following:

Say (Prophet Muhammad) to mankind, 'If you really love Allah, then follow me. Allah will love you and forgive you your sins, and Allah is the Oft-Forgiving, the Most Merciful.'[25]

---

[20] *Noble Quran*, 33:36
[21] *Noble Quran*, 5:55
[22] *Noble Quran*, 24:51
[23] *Noble Quran*, 4:64
[24] *Noble Quran*, 4:65
[25] *Noble Quran*, 3:31

15

Say (Prophet Muhammad), 'Follow that which has been sent down to you from your Lord, and follow not any guardian other than that.'[26]

(6) The Verse of Choosing:

And your Lord creates whatsoever He wills and chooses. No choice have they in any matter. Glorified be Allah, and Exalted above all that they associate as partners with Him.[27]

(7) The Verse of Judgment:

And Allah judges with truth, while those whom they invoke besides Him cannot judge anything. Certainly Allah is the All-Hearing, the All-Seeing.[28]

These examples from the Noble Quran show the characteristics of government which are only for Allah, the Exalted. The commonly repeated phrase "*a la lahu al-'amr wal-hukm*" (is not the command and the judgment His?) also illustrates this point. The most important characteristics of the leadership of Allah are the guardianship and the command, and He bestows this virtue on whomever He wills. The nature of the khilafah gives the khalifah the privilege to be a guardian over the people and obliges them to obey him. Since the absolute obedience and surrender is only for Allah, then only Allah the Almighty has the right to transfer this power and authority to whomever He wills.

Allah says, "O you who believe! Obey Allah, and obey the Messenger, and those vested with authority over you (*'ul ul-'amr minkum*). And if you quarrel about something, refer it to Allah and the Messenger."[29] But if a person assumes leadership and becomes a caliph or imam by power and intimidation then he will not

---

[26] *Noble Quran*, 7:3
[27] *Noble Quran*, 28:68
[28] *Noble Quran*, 40:20
[29] *Noble Quran*, 4:59

necessarily be entitled to be a legitimate Muslim leader. Logic dictates that the imam or caliph who succeeds the prophet should be appointed by Allah. Since Allah puts their obedience at the same level as obedience to Him and His Messenger, therefore not anyone is entitled to become the caliph of the prophet. Islamic history shows that some corrupt people assumed even the office of leadership and the khilafah during the Umayyad and Abbasid dynasties—then could this verse of obedience still apply to them? Would the believing Muslims have to follow these leaders blindly? Would Allah tell the Muslims to follow a corrupt leader and an oppressor?

In some of the hadith books, justification is found for such rulers to rule and a command for the Muslims to listen to them. Imam Bukhari narrates from the Prophet, "After me, there will be rulers (wilat), and you will find good ones and corrupt ones. You Muslims have to listen to both of them. Whoever breaks the unity of the whole (the jama'ah) will be considered outside of the religion of Islam."[30] Such a hadith is not compatible with the Noble Quran, which says, "And incline not towards those who do wrong (dhalamu) lest the Fire touch you and you have no protector other than Allah, nor will you be helped."[31] The Noble Quran clearly emphasizes that those who believe should neither support nor incline towards an oppressor at all. There is no way to justify paying allegiance to or endorsing an oppressor to be the caliph or leader of the Muslim nation (ummah); doing so, would be in gross violation of the Quranic injunctions. Verse 4:59 not only commands the faithful to obey the 'Ul ul-'amr or their legitimate guardians (who are the infallible imams) but it also rectifies their infallibility since no corrupt or wrongdoing person could be entitled by Allah to assume this trust.

---

[30] *Sahih al-Bukharim*, Kitab al-Imara, Hadith 1096, "The Book of Trials" Hadith 6530 and 6531, "Legal Judgments" Hadith 6610; *Sahih Muslim*, Kitab al-Imara, Hadith 3438; *Musnad* Ahmad ibn Hanbal, Part 1, 275, 297 and 310' al-Darami, *"The Book on Biographies"* Hadith 2407

[31] *Noble Quran*, 11:113

Imam Ali ibn Abi Talib

The Noble Quran and Prophet Muhammad specifically refer to the leadership of Imam Ali after the Prophet in several incidents.

Ghadir Khum

This incident took place on the 18th of Dhul Hijjah, the twelfth month of theu Islamic calendar, and has been narrated by 110 companions of the Prophet, 84 members of the following generation (the tabi'in), and 360 Muslim scholars from all schools of thought. Prophet Muhammad and approximately 114,000 of his companions had performed the farewell Hajj (pilgrimage) and were returning home. That year, during the Hajj, the weather was very hot with the blazing sun taking its toll on the pilgrims. When the Prophet arrived at Ghadir Khum, a marshland crossroads from which all the Muslims from different lands would part on their own ways, the Prophet stopped the caravan at noontime, and waited for those who were behind to arrive and called upon those who had gone ahead to return, for he had received a revelation from Allah which he had to deliver to the people. The revelation read, "O Messenger! Declare what has been revealed to you from Your Lord, and if you do not, then your mission will not have been fully declared, and Allah will protect you from the harm of the people."[1] Then the Prophet spoke

---

[1] *Noble Quran*, 5:67. See the following commentators (*mufassirin*): Tabari, Wahidi, Tha'alibi, Qurtubi, al-Razi, Ibn Kathir, Naysaburi, Suyuti, and Alusi al-Baghdadi, and the following historians: Balathari, Ibn Qutaybah, Tabari, al-Khatib al-Baghdadi, Ibn 'Abd al-Birr, Shahristani, Ibn Asakir, Ibn al-Athir, Ibn Abi al-Hadid, Ya'qut al-Hamawi, Ibn Khalaqan, Yafi'i, Ibn Kathir, Ibn Khuldun, al-Dhahabi, Ibn Hajar al-Askalani, Ibn al-Sabbagh al-Maliki, al-Maqrizi, and Jalal al-Din al-Suyuti, and also the following recorders of hadith: al-Shafi'i, Ahmad ibn Hanbal, Ibn Majah, Tirmidhi, Nisa'i, al-Baghawi, al-Dulabi, al-Tahawi,

a bit before asking the assembly whether he truly had authority over them or not. The people replied, "Yes, O Prophet, of course you are our leader (*mawla*)." He repeated this question three times, and the people responded in the same way each time, acknowledging his leadership. The Prophet then called for Ali, held up his arm so that their two arms formed one shape pointing upwards, and said to the people, "He whose leader (*mawla*) I am, Ali is his leader."

At that time, Ali was 33 years old. The people received this news with a variety of responses—some with happiness and some with resentment. The foremost to congratulate Ali were the future first and second caliphs; the second caliph said, "Congratulations, congratulations to you, O Ali; you have become my leader (*mawla*) and the leader of every faithful Muslim."[2]

After declaring the mentioned revelation another verse was revealed to Prophet Muhammad. Allah said, "Today I have completed for you the religion, and favored you with My bounty, and accepted Islam for you as the religion."[3] With this verse, the religion of Islam was completed by the appointment of Imam Ali to succeed the Prophet, and had he not been appointed as the successor, the religion of Islam would have been incomplete as is specifically mentioned in these verses.

The Verse of Warning (Indhar)

Three years after the advent of Islam, Allah commanded the Prophet to proclaim his invitation to Islam to his immediate family in Makkah by commanding, "And warn your tribe who are of near kindred."[4] The Prophet gathered forty members of his tribe, Bani Hashim and held a feast inside the house of his uncle Abu Talib by

---

Abu Ya'la al-Musali, al-Hakim al-Naysaburi, Khatib al-Khawarizmi, Muhibb al-Din al-Tabari, al-Dhahabi, and al-Muttaqi al-Hindi.

[2] Ahmad ibn Hanbal, *Musnad*, Vol. 4, 281; al-Ghazali, *Sirr al-'Alamin*, 12; al-Tabari, *al-Riyadh al-Nadhirah*, Vol. 2, 169

[3] *Noble Quran*, 5.3.

[4] *Noble Quran*, 26:214

preparing food for them. After they had finished eating, the Prophet said to them, "O children of 'Abd al-Mutallib! By Allah, I don't know any young person from among the Arabs who has brought his people something better than that which I am bringing you. I have brought you the best of this world and the next, and Allah has commanded me to invite you to it. So who will be my supporter in this endeavor, to be my brother, my successor (khalifah), and legatee?" No one stood up to accept this invitation except Ali ibn Abi Talib, who was only about 13 years old at the time, said, "I will be your supporter in this endeavor." The Prophet requested him to sit down and then repeated his question a second time. Again, only Ali stood up, and again the Prophet asked him to sit. When even the third time the Prophet heard no answer from the other family members, Ali stood up again and repeated his support. The Prophet then put his hand on his leg and said to the forty men from his immediate family, "This is my brother, my legatee, and my successor (khalifah) over you, so listen to him and obey him." The men stood and while laughing told the father of Ali, "Your nephew has ordered you to listen to your son and obey him."[5]

The Verse of Bowing (Ruku)

> Verily, your guardian (wali) is Allah, His messenger, and the believers; those who perform the prayers and give zakat (alms) while bowing down (in ruku).[6]

---

[5] *Ihqaq al-Haqq*, Vol. 4, 62; *Tarikh al-Tabari*, Vol. 2, 117; *Musnad* Ahmad ibn Hanbal, Vol. 1, 159; *Tarikh* Abul Fida, Vol. 1, 116; *Nadhm Durar al-Simtayn*, 82; *Kifayat al-Talib*, 205; *Tarikh Madinat Dimishq*, Vol.1, Hadith 87, 139 and 143; al-Hasakani, *Shawahid al-Tanzil*, Vol. 1, 420; Muhammad ibn Jarir al-Tabari, *Jami' al-Bayan*, Vol. 19, 131; Jalal al-Din al-Suyuti, *al-Durr al-Manthur*, Vol. 5, 97; *Tafsir ibn Kathir*, Vol. 3, 350; al-Baghdadi, *Tafsir al-Khazin*, Vol. 3, 371; al-Alusi al-Baghdadi, *Ruh al-Ma'ani*, Vol. 19, 122; al-Tantawi, *Tafsir al-Jawahir*, Vol. 13, 103; al-Hakim al-Naysaburi, *al-Mustadrak 'ala al-Sahihayn*, Vol. 3, 135. Other historical sources, such as *Sirat al-Halabi*, say that the Prophet added, "And he will be my minister (wazir) and inheritor (warith)."

[6] *Noble Quran*, 5:55

Numerous commentators of the Quran from all schools of thought identify the one referred to in this verse is Ali ibn Abi Talib. The famous commentator, Zamakhshari says about this verse, "It was revealed in favor of Ali (may Allah enlighten his face). When a beggar asked him for alms in the masjid and Ali was in the position of ruku during the prayers, he gave away his ring while in that position. It seems it was loose on the little finger, for he did not exert any effort in taking it off, which would have nullified his prayer. If you ask how it could be in favor of Ali since the wording is in the plural form, I would say that the form is plural although its instigator is a single man to encourage people to follow his example and earn a similar reward; and also to draw attention to the fact that the believers must be extremely mindful and benevolent towards the poor such that if a situation can not be postponed until after the prayer, then it should not be delayed until having finished it."[7]

Similarly, al-Wahidi in his book on the commentary of the Quran entitled, *Asbab al-Nuzul*, cites Kalbi's narration, that the cause of this revelation was Imam Ali. Kalbi says, "The later part of this verse is in favor of Ali ibn Abi Talib (may Allah be gracious to him) because he gave his ring to a beggar while in the state of *ruku* during the prayers."[8] Many other commentaries also hold that this verse refers to Imam Ali including: *Sunan al-Nisa'i, Tafsir al-Kabir* by Tha'alibi, *Musnad Ahmad ibn Hanbal*,[9] *Musnad ibn Marduwayh*, and *Kanz al-'Ummal*.[10]

The Verse of Guardianship

O you who believe! Obey Allah, and obey the Messenger, and those vested with authority over you (*'Ul ul-'amr minkum*). And if you quarrel about

---

[7] Zamakhshari, *Tafsir al-Kashif* (See interpretation of ch. 5 v. 55)
[8] Wahidi, *Asbab al-Nuzul*, (See interpretation of ch. 5 v. 55)
[9] *Noble Quran*, 5:38
[10] Vol. 6, Hadith 391 and 5991

something, then refer it to Allah and the Messenger.[11]

By the explanation from the Prophet Muhammad, this verse is also one of the Quranic references to the leadership of Imam Ali after the Prophet, and it necessitates the obedience of the faithful to Allah, the Prophet, and those vested with authority over them. When this verse was revealed to the Prophet, one of his great companions, Jabir ibn 'Abdullah al-Ansari asked:

> O Prophet of Allah! We know Allah and His Messenger, but who are 'those vested with authority over you' ('Ul ul-'amr) whose obedience Allah considers equal to that of Allah and the Prophet? The Prophet replied that those are my successors and the leaders of the Muslims after me. The first of them is Ali ibn Abi Talib, then al-Hassan and al-Husayn, then Ali ibn al-Husayn, then Muhammad ibn Ali, who is known as al-Baqir. You, Jabir will see him and when you see him, give him my salam.[12] Then al-Sadiq Ja'far ibn Muhammad, then Musa ibn Ja'far, then Ali ibn Musa, then Muhammad ibn Ali, then Ali ibn Muhammad, then al-Hassan ibn Ali, then the one who bears my name, Muhammad. And he will be the proof (hujjah) of Allah on the earth.

Prophetic Narrations Appointing Imam Ali as Successor

Prophet Muhammad told the Muslims both about the succession of the designated members of his family (Ahlul Bayt), which will be dealt with in the next section, as well as the specific succession of Imam Ali. The Messenger of Allah has been recorded to have said in regards to Imam Ali:

---

[11] Noble Quran, 4:59
[12] i.e. peaceful greeting or greetings of peace.

You are in the same position with relation to me as Aaron was with Moses, except that there will be no prophet after me.[13]

He who wishes to live as I have lived and to die as I will die, and enter the Garden of Eternal Bliss which Allah has promised me—let him take Ali as his leader (*wali*), because Ali will never lead you away from the Path of Truth, nor will he take you into error.[14]

Ali is the authority (*wali*) over every believer (*mu'min*) after me.[15]

Ali is the doorway to my knowledge, and after me he will explain to my followers what has been sent to me. Love for Ali is faith, and spite towards him is hypocrisy.[16]

I am the city of knowledge, and Ali is its gate. He who wishes to reach this city should enter through its gate.[17]

Ali is from me, and I am from Ali, and none delivers except me and Ali.[18]

---

[13] *Sahih al-Bukhari*, "Book on Outstanding Traits" Hadith 3430, "Battles" Hadith 4064; *Sahih Muslim*, "Book of the Merits of the Companions" Hadith 4418; al-Tirmidhi, "Book on Outstanding Traits" Hadith 3664; Ibn Majah, "Book on the Introduction" 112 and 118; *Musnad* Ahmad ibn Hanbal, Vol.1, 173, 175, 177, 179, 182, 184, and 185.

[14] al-Hakim, *al-Mustadrak*, Vol. 3, 128; al-Muttaqi al-Hindi, *Kanz al-Ummal*, Vol. 6, 155

[15] *Musnad* Ahmad ibn Hanbal, Vol. 5, 25; *Sahih Tirmidhi*, Vol. 5, 296

[16] *Kanz al-Ummal*, al-Muttaqi al-Hindi, Vol. 6, 170

[17] al-Hakim, *al-Mustadrak*, Vol. 3, 226; Ibn Jarir, *Kanz al-Ummal*; al-Muttaqi al-Hindi, Vol. 15, 13; *Tarikh ibn Kathir*, Vol. 7, 358

[18] *Sunan* ibn Majah, Vol. 1, 44; *Sahih Tirmidhi*, Vol. 5, 300

He who obeys me will have obeyed Allah, and he who disobeys me will have disobeyed Allah. And he who obeys Ali will have obeyed me, and he who disobeys Ali will have disobeyed me.[19]

At the Battle of Khaybar the Muslims were struggling to conquer the castle. The two companions, Abu Bakr and Umar had previously failed in their attempts to defeat the enemies, at which the Messenger of Allah said, I will certainly give this standard (i.e. flag) to a man whom Allah and His Messenger love." Other narrations say that the Prophet said, "Allah will grant victory through the one who loves Allah and His Messenger." In either case, the Prophet Muhammad gave the standard to Ali, and Allah granted victory through his hand.[20]

Twelve Leaders to Succeed the Prophet

In addition to the specific narrations emphatically identifying Imam Ali as the successor of the Prophet Muhammad, the Prophet was also recorded to have said on numerous occasions that after him he would be succeeded by twelve leaders from his tribe of Quraysh. Some of these narrations are:

The caliphate will remain among the Quraysh even if only two people are left (on the earth).[21]

I joined the company of the Prophet with my father and heard him say, "This caliphate will not end

---

[19] al-Hakim, Vol. 3, 221, al-Dhahabi

[20] *Sahih al-Bukhari*, "Book of Jihad and Marching" Hadith 2724 and 2753, "Battles" Hadith 3888; *Sahih Muslim*, "Book on the Merits of the Companions" Hadith 4423-4424; *Musnad* Ahmad ibn Hanbal, Vol. 5, 333

[21] *Sahih al-Bukhari*, "Book on Outstanding Traits", Hadith 3240; *Sahih Muslim*, Kitab al-Imarah, Hadith 3392; *Musnad* Ahmad ibn Hanbal, Part 2. 29, 93, and 128

until there have come the twelve caliphs among
them." The narrator said, "Then he (the Prophet)
said something which I could not follow." I said to
my father, "What did he say?" He said, "He has said,
'all of them will be from Quraysh.'"[22]

Nevertheless, extensive research show that the accurate version
of the Prophet's narration is that 'all of them will be from Bani
Hashim,' which is exclusive to the imams of Ahlul Bayt.

Who are the Twelve Leaders?

The Prophet said:

I and Ali are the fathers of this nation. He who
recognizes us as such believes in Allah, the Mighty
and Glorious. And from Ali are my two
grandchildren, Hassan and Husayn, each of whom
is a prince over the youth in Heaven; and among
the descendants of Husayn are nine. Obedience to
them is obedience to me, and disobedience to them
is disobedience to me. The ninth of them is the
Qa'im (the firmly established) and Mahdi—the
executor and the one divinely trained for right
guidance.[23]

Stated to his grandson Husayn when he was only a few
years old, the Prophet said to him:

You are a sayyid (master) and the son of a sayyid.
You are an imam and the son of an imam, the
brother of an imam and the father of imams. You
are Allah's proof and confirmation and the son of

---

[22] *Sahih al-Bukhari*, "Book on Legal Judgments" Hadith 6682; *Sahih Muslim*,
Kitab al-Imarah, Hadith 3393; *al-Tirmidhi*, "Book on the Trials" Hadith
2149; *Abu Dawud*, "Book on al-Mahdi" Hadith 3731; *Musnad* Ahmad ibn
Hanbal, Vol. 5, 87, 90, 92, 95, 97, 99-101, and 106-108
[23] *Ikmal al-Din*

His proof. You are the father of nine of Allah's proofs in your line of descendants. The ninth of them is the *Qa'im* (the firmly established, the executor).[24]

---

[24] Ibid.,

The Ahlul Bayt

The best way to introduce the *Ahlul Bayt* to the Muslim nation is to recall what the Noble Quran says about them. Several verses of the Noble Quran refer specifically to the virtues of the Ahlul Bayt and their outstanding position in Islam. Whenever the Noble Quran refers to the Ahlul Bayt, it refers to a specific group of people who were related not only by blood, but more importantly, by ideology and faith to the Prophet. However, it **does not** refer to all of his blood relations, his friends or his wives.

The Verse of Purity (Taharah)

> Allah only desires to keep away uncleanliness from you, O People of the House (Ahlul Bayt), and to make you as pure as possible.[1]

The prominent scholars of Islam and the narrators of the Prophetic tradition unanimously agree that Ahlul Bayt (the household of the Prophet) which Almighty Allah uses in the above verse of the Noble Quran refers to the daughter of the Prophet Muhammad, Lady Fatima al-Zahra, his cousin, Ali ibn Abi Talib, and their children Hassan and Husayn.[2] Tabarani narrates from one of the respected wives of the Prophet, Um Salamah that the Messenger of Allah once told his daughter, Lady Fatima to call her husband Ali and their two sons, Hassan and Husayn. When they came, the Messenger of Allah covered them with a cloak, put his hand on them and said, "O Allah, these are *Al-e*-Muhammad (the family of Muhammad), so shower Your blessings and favors upon *Al-e*-Muhammad just as You showered them on *Al-e*-Ibrahim. You are the Praiseworthy, the Glorious." Um Salamah says that she raised the

---

[1] *Noble Quran,* 33:33
[2] al-Suyuti, *al-Durr al-Manthur*

cloak to join them, but the Prophet took it from her hand saying, "You are also on the right."[3]

Although the beginning of verse 33:33 addresses the wives of the Prophet and continues to address them up until the middle part of the verse, but upon reaching "Ahlul Bayt" it excludes them.[4] The previous and subsequent statements which are directed towards the wives of the Prophet are in the feminine pronouns and gender, but this verse referring to the Ahlul Bayt is in the masculine or mixed gender; thus it makes it clear that it is not addressed to the wives of the Prophet. However, even without the grammatical evidence, the relationship between some of the wives of the Prophet does not fit the spirit of this verse which asserts the physical, mental, and spiritual purity of the family of the Prophet Muhammad.

To emphasize that the phrase "Ahlul Bayt" in this verse refers only to five people—Prophet Muhammad, Ali, Lady Fatima, Hassan, and Husayn—narrators say that whenever the Prophet used to pass by his daughter, Lady Fatima's house on the way to the masjid for the dawn prayers he would stop there and proclaim, "Come to prayer, O Ahlul Bayt, to prayer. Allah desires to keep away uncleanliness from you, O Ahlul Bayt, and to make you as pure as possible."[5] Imam Anas ibn Malik adds that the Prophet did this for six months every day on his way for his morning prayers at the masjid.[6]

---

[3] Tirmidhi, *Manaqib Ahlul-Bayt*, Vol. 2, 308

[4] It is not uncommon to find a group of verses discussing one theme and having one verse in the middle that discusses another theme. For example see Quran, Surah 5, verse 3 and Surah 5, v. 66-68.

[5] Ibn Mardawayh. Ahmad ibn Hanbal. Tirmidhi. Ibn Mundir. Tabarani. For more details see: Tabataba'i, *al-Mizan*.

[6] al-Miqrizi, *Fadha'il Ahlul-Bayt*, 21

The Verse of Affection (Muwaddah)

> Say, I do not ask from you any reward for it
> (preaching the message) but love for my relatives
> (*qurba* which here refers to the *Ahlul Bayt*[7]).[8]

When explaining this verse, Fakhr al-Din al-Razi says, "Without doubt, no one was as near to the Prophet as Lady Fatima, Ali, Hassan, and Husayn. This is a well-known fact for all the chains of narration, that these were his '*al*'." Thus, '*al*' or '*ahl*' refers only to the immediate family of the Prophet—namely: Lady Fatima, Ali, Hassan, and Husayn.

Some argue that Hassan and Husayn were not the sons of the Prophet because they were the sons of Imam Ali. According to old Arab custom, the mother was considered as only a means to deliver a child, but nonetheless, their direct lineage to the Prophet is through their mother, Lady Fatima al-Zahra. It has been narrated that the 'Abbasid caliph Harun al-Rashid asked the seventh Imam of the school of Ahlul Bayt, Imam Musa ibn Ja'far how he could attribute himself to the Prophet while he was the child of Ali and Lady Fatima – thus, how could he be related to the Prophet? The Imam then cited to him a verse that refers to the descendants of Prophet Abraham (Ibrahim), "And from his progeny were David (Dawud), Solomon (Sulayman), Job (Ayyub), Joseph (Yusuf), Moses (Musa), and Aaron (Harun)—thus do We reward the good-doers—and Zachariah (Zakariyya), and John (Yahya), and Jesus (Isaa), and Elias (Ilyas)—each one of them was of the righteous."[9] The Imam then asked the caliph who the father of Isaa (Jesus) was. Harun answered that he was fatherless. The Imam replied, "Then you can see that Allah linked him to Ibrahim through his mother, Mary and

---

[7] Ibn Hajar, *Sawa'iq*. Vol.11, 160; *Tabaqat al-Kubra,* Ibn Sa'ad; *Sahih Muslim*; *Musnad* Ahmad ibn Hanbal; *Tafsir al-Durr al-Manthur*

[8] *Noble Quran,* 42:23

[9] *Noble Quran,* 6:84-85

Allah did the same for us, linking us to Prophet Muhammad through our mother Lady Fatima al-Zahra."[10]

In many instances, the Prophet refers to Lady Fatima with intense love and affection, such as when he says, "Fatima is a part of me. Her happiness is my happiness, and her pain is my pain." The Prophet would also point towards the children of Fatima - Hassan and Husayn - and say on many occasions, "These are my sons," or "This is my son." That is why the community of the companions in Madina referred to both Hassan and Husayn as the 'sons of Prophet Muhammad.'

The Verse of Malediction (Mubahilah)

> But whoever disputes with you in this matter after what has come to you of knowledge, then say, 'Come, let us call our sons and your sons, and our women and your women, and ourselves and yourselves, and let us beseech Allah and invoke His curse upon the liars.'[11]

This milestone event in the Islamic history has been narrated by all the historians, narrators, and commentators of the Quran. It is an event which reveals the exalted status of the Family of the Prophet. The narrations say that a delegation of Christians from Najran came to the city of Madina in order to meet with the Prophet to discuss his prophethood and the religion he was preaching. The Prophet proved to them that Jesus (Isa) was the son of Mary; he was a human being, a Prophet, and a servant of Allah as the Quran states and that regarding him as the son of God is blasphemy, since Allah, the Exalted is much higher than such human characteristics. After discussing these points extensively, the Prophet found them still deliberately persisting in their false beliefs and traditions—namely on the deification of Prophet Jesus—thus, Allah revealed the verse, which was a major challenge to the Christians, to pray and invoke

---

[10] Tabarsi, *al-Ihtijaj*, Vol. 2, Argument 271 and 335
[11] *Noble Quran*, 3:61

upon Allah that a curse may overtake the party that insists on falsehood. Early the next morning, on the 24th of the lunar month of Dhul al-Hijjah, in accordance with Allah's command, the Prophet arrived at the meeting carrying Husayn in his arms, while holding Hassan by the hand, followed by his beloved daughter, Lady Fatima and behind them was his son-in-law and cousin, Ali ibn Abi Talib carrying the banner of Islam. Seeing that the Prophet was accompanied only by his immediate family, the Christians were convinced that he was truthful otherwise he would have never dared to bring his dearest kin along with him. The Christian delegation backed away from the malediction argument and returned back to Najran.

Zamakhshari, in his *Tafsir al-Kashshaf*, narrates the event as:

> When this verse was revealed, the Prophet invited the Christians to the malediction, to invoke the curse of Allah upon the liars. The Christians held a discourse among themselves tmhat night in which their leader, 'Abd al-Masih stated his views. He said, "O Christians, know that Muhammad is a God-sent Prophet who has brought you the final message from your Lord. By God, no nation ever dared to challenge a Prophet with malediction but that woe befell them. Not only will they perish, but their children will also be afflicted by the curse." Saying this—that it is better to reach a compromise with the Prophet rather than challenge his truth and perish—'Abd al-Masih advised his party to stop hostilities and retain their religion by submitting to the Prophet's terms. "So if you persist (for a confrontation) we will all perish. But if you, to keep your faith, refuse (to have a showdown) and remain as you are, then make peace with the man (the Prophet) and return to your land." The next day, the Prophet, carrying Husayn in his arms, leading Hassan by the hand, followed by his daughter Lady

Fatima, behind whom came Ali, entered the appointed place and the Prophet was heard saying to his family, "When I invoke Allah, second the invocation." The pontiff of Najran, upon seeing the Prophet and his family, addressed the Christians, "O Christians! I am witnessing such faces that if God wishes, for their sake, He would move mountains for them. Do not accept their challenge for malediction, for if you do, you would all perish and there will not remain any Christians on the face of the earth till the Day of Resurrection."[12] Heeding his advice, the Christians said to the Prophet, "O Abul-Qasim, we have decided not to hold malediction with you. You keep your religion, and we will keep ours." The Prophet told them, "If you refuse to hold malediction, then submit to Allah, and you will receive what the Muslims receive and contribute what the Muslims contribute." The Christians delegates, saying that they had no desire to fight the Muslims, proposed a treaty asking for peace which the Prophet of Islam accepted.

---

[12] *Musnad* Ahmad ibn Hanbal, Vol. 1, 185; Tabari, *Tafsir*, Vol. 3, 192; al-Hakim, *al-Mustadrak*, Vol. 3, 150; al-Hafiz Abu Nu'aym, *Dala'il al-Nubuwwah*, 297; al-Naysaburi, *Asbab al-Nuzul*, 74; Abu Bakr ibn al-'Arabi, *Ahkam al-Quran*, Vol. 1, 115; al-Fakhr al-Razi, *Tafsir al-Kabir*, Vol. 8, 85; al-Juzri, *Usd al-Ghabah*, Vol. 4, 25; Ibn al-Jawzi, *Tadhkira Sibt*, 17; Qurtubi, *al-Jami' li-Ahkam al-Quran*, Vol. 3, 104; *Tafsir ibn Kathir*, Vol. 1, 370; Ibn Kathir, *al-Bidayah wal-Nihayah*, Vol. 5, 52; Ibn Hajar al-Asqalani, *al-Isabah*, Vol. 2, 503; Ibn al-Sabbagh al-Maliki, *al-Fusul al-Muhimmah*, 108; Jalal al-Din al-Suyuti, *al-Durr al-Manthur*, Vol. 4, 38; Jalal al-Din al-Suyuti, *Tarikh al-Khulafa'*, 115; Ibn Hajar, *al-Sawa'iq al-Muhriqa*, 199; Altogether 47 narrators and commentators of the Noble Quran from the four schools of thought narrate that the immediate family of the Prophet were only Lady Fatima, Ali, Hassan, and Husayn.

Although other women were present in the family of the Prophet at that time, all the commentators, narrators, and historians agree that in reference to the Quranic verse, "our women" referred only to Lady Fatima al-Zahra, "our children" referred only to Hassan and Husayn, and "ourselves" referred only to the Prophet and Imam Ali.

The Verse of Prayer (Salat)

> Surely Allah and His angels bless the Prophet. O you
> who believe, call for divine blessings upon him, and
> salute him with a becoming salutation.[13]

In the five obligatory prayers, during the *tashhahud* (testimony), those offering their prayers must salute the Prophet and his progeny—a term exclusively reserved for Ali, Lady Fatima, Hassan, Husayn, and their righteous descendants. The emphasis on the Prophet's family in salutation is another indication of their pivotal position after the Prophet. By asking the believers to exalt these noble personalities, Allah, the Almighty reminds the Muslim nation that He has chosen the Ahlul Bayt for the role of leading the Muslim nation.

One of the most prominent commentators of the Quran, Fakhr al-Din al-Razi narrates the response of the Prophet when he was asked by some of his companions how to send blessings upon him. He said, "Say, 'O Allah, send blessings on Muhammad and on the progeny of Muhammad as you sent blessings on Ibrahim and on the progeny of Ibrahim. And send grace on Muhammad and on the progeny of Muhammad just as you sent grace on Ibrahim and on the progeny of Ibrahim. You are the Praiseworthy, the Glorious.'"[14] Al-Razi comments that if Allah and His angels send their blessings upon the Prophet, then what need is there for our blessings? He answers his own question by saying that when we send blessings on the Prophet Muhammad it is not because he is in need of them, because

---

[13] *Noble Quran*, 33:56
[14] *Tafsir al-Kabir*, Vol. 3, 56

he already has the blessings of Allah and thus, he does not even require the blessings of the angels. When we send blessings on him, we send them to glorify Allah and also to reveal our gratitude towards Allah such that He may have compassion on us and reward us. Thus, the Prophet says, "Whoever sends blessings on me once, Allah will send blessings on him ten times."

Another verse in the Noble Quran asserts the same teaching when Allah the Almighty sends His blessings on the family of the Prophet by saying, "Peace be upon the Al-e-Yasin!"[15] According to some commentators, "Yasin" is one of the names of the Prophet, as stated in Surah (chapter) *Ya Sin* when it addresses the Prophet as, "*Yasin*, by the Quran full of wisdom, truly you are one of the messengers...."[16]

The Verse of Feeding

> Truly, the righteous drink of a cup tempered with camphor, a fountain from which the servants of Allah drink, flowing in abundance. They (the Family of the Prophet) fulfill vows and fear a Day, the evil of which is widespread. And they give food out of love for Him to the poor and the orphan and the captive. 'We feed you for Allah's sake and pleasure only. We desire from you neither reward nor thanks. Surely, we fear from our Lord a stern, distressful Day,' so Allah will ward off from them the evil of that Day and cause them to meet with splendor and happiness and reward them for their steadfastness with a garden and with silk.[17]

Surah 76 in the Noble Quran descended to honor a sacred gesture performed by the Ahlul Bayt. Allah entitled this Surah, Insan (*Mankind*) to draw attention of the people to the beauty of

---

[15] *Noble Quran*, 37:130
[16] Ibn Hajar, *al-Sawa'iq*, Ch. 11
[17] *Noble Quran*, 76:5-13

mankind's deeds on earth, and to tell them that they should not be selfish or greedy; rather, they should be caring and thoughtful people who spend their time thinking of other human beings around them. The chapter begins, "Has there not been over man a period of time when he was nothing to be mentioned? Verily, We and created man from drops of mixed semen in order to try him, so We made him hearing, seeing. Verily, We showed him the way, whether he be grateful or ungrateful."

This introduction prepares our minds for the big sacrifice of the Family of the Prophet—Ali, Lady Fatima, Hassan, Husayn, and their maidservant Fiddah. The incident provoking these verses began when Hassan and Husayn fell ill, and Lady Fatima al-Zahra asked her father what to do. The Prophet advised her to make a vow with Allah that if He cured them then the entire family would fast for three days. Hassan and Husayn were cured, and the process of fasting began. At that time there was nothing in their house to eat, so Imam Ali went to a Khaybarian Jew named Shimon and borrowed three measures of barley. His wife, Lady Fatima milled one measure into flour and baked it into five loaves of bread, one for each of them. Ali, Lady Fatima, and their two sons, Hassan and Husayn along with their maidservant Fiddah fasted for three consecutive days. On the first day, at the time of breaking the fast, a destitute (*miskin*) person came to the door asking for some food. They took the food they intended to eat—a loaf of bread each—and gave it to him. They then broke their fast only with water. On the second day, at the time of breaking their fast, an orphan came to their door, and they again gave him all their food. On the third day, at the time of breaking the fast, a prisoner of war (a non-Muslim who had been captured in the defensive wars of Islam and was living in the city of Madina) came to their door and asked for some food, and again, they took all five loaves of bread and gave it to the man, breaking their fast for the third consecutive day with only water. Afterwards, the Messenger of Allah made a visit and saw his daughter, Lady Fatima al-Zahra and her two children, Hassan and Husayn were pale and too weak to speak, and he saw that they were trembling from hunger. Lady

37

Fatima herself was sitting hollow-eyed on her prayer mat, her stomach sunk into her back. As he was asking them the reason for their state, angel Jibril (Gabriel) immediately came to the Prophet with Surah 76, "O Muhammad, Allah congratulates you for the sacrifice of your household."[18]

These verses not only translate the generosity and steadfastness of the Ahlul Bayt but also reveal the total submission of the Family of the Prophet and their immaculate and pure personalities. Commentators of the Quran have a consensus that these verses speak of the Ahlul Bayt and place them at the highest level of piety and show them as models for the generosity of mankind. Humanity would be rightly guided if they followerd their parable.

The Verse of Guardianship

> O you who believe! Obey Allah, and obey the Messenger, and those vested with authority over you ('ul ul-'amr minkum). And if you quarrel about something, refer it to Allah and the Messenger.[19]

This verse, as explained in the previous section, refers to the guardianship of Imam Ali, and subsequently, the rest of the Ahlul Bayt. The Prophet has said about "those vested with authority over you," that "They are my successors and the leaders of the Muslims after me. The first of them is Ali ibn Abi Talib, then al-Hassan and al-Husayn, then Ali ibn al-Husayn, then Muhammad ibn Ali, who is known as al-Baqir, then al-Sadiq Ja'far ibn Muhammad, then Musa ibn Ja'far, then Ali ibn Musa, then Muhammad ibn Ali, then Ali ibn Muhammad, then al-Hassan ibn Ali, then the one who bears my name—Muhammad. And he will be the proof (hujjah) of Allah on the earth."[20]

---

[18] Zamakhshari, *Tafsir al-Kashhaf*, Ch. 76; Fakhr al-Razi, *Tafsir al-Kabir*, Ch. 76; Tabarsi, *Mu'jam al-Bayan*, Ch. 76

[19] *Noble Quran*, 4:59

[20] *Tafsir al-Burhan*

The Hadith of the Two Weighty Things (Thaqalayn)

> It is probable that I will be called soon, and I will
> respond. So I leave behind me two weighty (very
> worthy and important) things, the Book of Allah
> (the Quran), which is a string stretched from the
> heaven to the earth; and my progeny, my Ahlul
> Bayt. Verily Allah, the Merciful, the Aware, has
> informed me that these two will never be separated
> from each other until they meet me at the Fountain
> of Abundance (the *Hawdh* of *Kawthar*, a spring in
> heaven). Therefore, be careful of how you treat
> these two in my absence, said the Messenger of
> Allah.[21]

This hadith was declared on, at least five occasions—the first
being the farewell speech during the last hajj, the second at Ghadir
Khum, the third after the Prophet left the city of Ta'if near Makkah,
the fourth at the pulpit in Madina, and the fifth—just before he
died—in his room which was full of his companions.

Given the high importance of the Noble Quran, why would the
Prophet associate the Ahlul Bayt with the Noble Quran and place
them second in importance to it? The answer is that Ahlul Bayt are
the best to explain the true meaning and interpretation of this
Noble Book. The Noble Quran, as it states itself, contains both clear
(*muhkam*) and unclear (*mutashabiah*) verses, and so the correct
interpretation of these unclear verses must be passed on from the
Prophet himself, as he did to his Ahlul Bayt. In addition, the Ahlul
Bayt, due to their closeness to the Prophet, had an unparalleled
knowledge of his traditions.

---

[21] This hadith has been narrated by more than twenty companions of the
Prophet and has also been narrated by over 185 narrators mentioned in
Sahih Muslim, Vol. 2, 238; *Musnad* Ahmad ibn Hanbal, Vol. 5, 181-182;
Sahih Tirmidhi, Vol. 2, 220.

Similar Narrations from the Prophet Muhammad about his Ahlul Bayt

The parable of my Ahlul Bayt is similar to that of Noah's ark. Whoever embarks it will certainly be rescued, but the one who opposes boarding it will certainly be drowned.[22]

Just like the stars protect mankind from losing its way in travel, so are my Ahlul Bayt; they are the safeguard against discord in matters of religion.[23]

Acknowledgement of the Al-e-Muhammad means salvation from the Hellfire; the love of Al-e-Muhammad is a passport for crossing the bridge of Sirat; and obedience to Al-e-Muhammad is protection from divine wrath.[24]

---

[22] This hadith has been narrated by eight companions of the Prophet and eight disciples of the companions, by sixty well-known scholars and more than ninety authors from the brothers of the Sunni school, such as Ahmad ibn Hanbal, Mishkat al-Masabih, 523; Fara'id al-Simtayn, Vol. 2, 242; al-Sawa'iq al-Muhriqah, 234; 'Uyun al-Akhbar, Vol. 1, 211.

[23] al-Hakim, al-Mustadrak (quoting Ibn 'Abbas), Vol. 3, 149

[24] al-Shafa, Vol 2, 40

Infallibility

The Shi'a school of thought maintains the belief that all the prophets of Allah, from Adam to Muhammad, as well as the twelve successors (imams) of the Prophet Muhammad, and his daughter, Lady Fatima al-Zahra were infallible throughout their entire lives and never committed any type of sin that would earn the displeasure of Allah. The clearest way to see this point is to consider that these people were the examples sent for humanity to follow, and thus, if they committed errors then people would be obliged to follow their errors, thereby rendering the prophets and messengers unreliable.

Infallibility means protection. In Islamic terminology it means the spiritual grace of Allah enabling a person to abstain from sins by his/her own free will. The power of infallibility or without sin does not make a person incapable of committing sins, rather he/she refrains from sins and mistakes by his/her own power and will.

Infallibility is essential for the prophets and messengers because their job is not only to convey the divine scriptures of Allah but also to lead and guide humanity towards the right path. Therefore, they must be role models and perfect examples for all of mankind. Both the Noble Quran and conventional wisdom illustrate this point; the Noble Quran mentions infallibility thirteen times. Allah says to Satan, "Certainly you shall have no authority over My servants except those who follow you and go astray."[1] Satan thus replied to Allah, "By Your might, I will surely mislead all of them, except Your chosen servants among them (the messengers and the imams)."[2]

---

[1] *Noble Quran*, 15:42
[2] *Noble Quran*, 38:82

There are some verses in the Noble Quran which might imply that some of the prophets (such as Adam, Musa (Moses), or Yunus (Jonah)) committed sins. As for Prophet Adam, he did not disobey the obligatory commands of Allah; the command that he did not honor was a recommended one, not a mandatory one and so—according to Islamic terminology—he did not commit a sin. When speaking about the "disobedience" of Prophet Adam, the Noble Quran does not mean disobedience in the literal term; it means that it was not expected from a person like Prophet Adam, who was a leader for humanity, not to adhere to Allah's advisory commands. Therefore, such an act is labeled allegorically as a sin in the Noble Quran. "And indeed We made a covenant with Adam before, but he forgot, and We found on his part no firm will-power ('azm)." His guilt was that he did not demonstrate will-power, not that he violated Allah's rules because the commands were advisory and not obligatory. As a result of his behavior, he was to lose the privilege granted to him, "Verily, you have a promise from Us that you will never be hungry therein, nor naked, and you will not suffer from thirst therein, nor suffer from the sun's heat."[3]

As for Prophet Musa, the Noble Quran says about him saying the following, "And they have a charge of crime against me, and I fear that they will kill me."[4] This charge came about when he pushed a man and inadvertently killed him. At that time, Prophet Musa was defending one of his tribesmen, and when he pushed the man from the people of Pharaoh it happened that the man was so weak that he fell to the ground and died. Prophet Musa did not intend to kill him, and thus he fled the scene because he did not want to fall captive to Pharaoh and his army, which was searching for him. When Prophet Musa speaks of them having a "charge of crime" against him, he is reiterating the accusations of the Pharaoh's people, not necessarily believing that those accusations are true.

---

[3] *Noble Quran,* 20:118-119
[4] *Noble Quran,* 26:14

The case of Prophet Yunus (Jonah) is similar. The Quran says, "And remember, when he went off in anger, and he imagined that We would not confine him. But he cried through the darkness, saying, 'There is no Lord except You. Glory be to You! Surely, I have been one of those who did injustice to their own souls.'"[5] In this case, Prophet Yunus meant that he had been wrong to himself, but wrongdoing one's self is neither a sin nor a mistake. His "wrongdoing to himself" was being impatient with his followers and fleeing from them when they persisted in rejecting his call to worship Allah. They ridiculed him and thus he left them to face their grave destiny.

Most of the verses of the Noble Quran which might imply that the Prophet Muhammad committed a sin have deeper hermeneutic interpretations. Not all of the verses of the Quran are meant to be taken literally; in-fact deeper meaning lies behind many of them. "It is He who has sent down to you the Book. In it are verses which are entirely clear. They are the foundations of the book. And (there are) others that are not entirely clear (i.e. allegorical); so as for those in whose hearts there is a deviation, they follow that which is not entirely clear thereof, seeking dispute (*fitna*) and seeking to distort the true meaning. But none knows the hidden meanings save Allah and those firmly grounded in knowledge (the Prophet and the Ahul-Bayt)."[6] Furthermore, the character and general respect accorded to the Prophet shows without any doubt that he was not one of the wrongdoers.

Inappropriate narrations are found in some books of hadith regarding violations committed by various prophets of Allah. For example, Imam al-Bukhari narrates:

> Umar sought permission from the Messenger of Allah to visit him when some women of Quraysh were busy talking with him and raising their voices

---

[5] *Noble Quran*, 21:87
[6] *Noble Quran*, 3:7

above his voice. When Umar sought permission, they stood up and went hurriedly behind the curtain. The Messenger of Allah gave him permission smilingly. Thereupon Umar said, 'O Messenger of Allah, may Allah keep you happy all your life.' Then the Messenger of Allah said, 'I wonder at those women who were with me, and that no sooner did they hear your voice that they immediately wore the hejab.'[7]

Similarly, Imam Muslim narrates about the Noble Prophet as follows:

Abu Bakr came to see me and I had two girls with me from among the girls of the Ansar, and they were singing what the Ansar recited to one another at the Battle of Bu'ath. They were not however singing girls. Upon (seeing) this, Abu Bakr said, 'What? This wind instrument of Satan (being played) in the house of the Messenger of Allah, and this too on Eid (Muslim holiday) day?' At this, the Messenger of Allah said, 'Abu Bakr, all people have a festival, and this is our festival (so let them play on).'[8]

---

[7] *Sahih al-Bukhari*, "Book on the Beginning of Creation" Hadith 3051, "Book on Outstanding Traits" Hadith 3407, "Good Manners" Hadith 5621; *Sahih Muslim*, "Book on the Merits of the Companions" Hadith 4410; *Musnad* Ahmad ibn Hanbal, Vol. 1, 171, 182, and 187

[8] *Sahih al-Bukhari*, "Book on Friday Prayer" Hadith 897; *Sahih Muslim*, "Book on the 'Eid Prayers" Hadith 1479; al-Nisa'i, "Book on the 'Eid Prayers" Hadith 1575-1577 and 1579; *Sunan* ibn Majah, "Book on Marriage" Hadith 1888; *Musnad* Ahmad ibn Hanbal, Part 6, 166, 186, and 247

It has also been narrated that the Prophet Muhammad was seen standing and urinating in public.[9] Clearly, acts which the first and second caliphs and the laymen alike would consider un-Islamic would not have been done openly by the Prophet of Allah. No Muslim would accept such behavior from the leader of humanity whose example the Noble Quran commands to be followed in all aspects.

In the books of hadith, there are other unreliable narrations which contradict wisdom and common sense.

There are similar narrations also about some of the other prophets of Allah, for example:

> The Angel of Death came to Musa and said, 'Respond to (the call of) Allah (i.e. be prepared for death).' Musa gave a blow to the eye of the Angel of Death and knocked it out. The Angel went back to Allah and said, 'You sent me to Your servant who does not want to die, for look he knocked out my eye.' Allah then restored his eye.[10]

If an ordinary Muslim person attacked someone who was doing his duty, then he would be called an abuser, and an offender and charges would be brought against him. Thus, such behavior is completely unbelievable and unacceptable especially if that person is one of the five universal prophets sent to guide, enlighten, and educate people by their fine examples and morality. Why would one, such as Prophet Musa attack the Angel of Death who came to bring him closer to Allah? Narrations like this one are completely not authentic or acceptable. Muslims must open their eyes to such

---

[9] *Sahih Muslim*, Bab al-Hirab wal-Darq Yawm al-'Eid; *Sahih Muslim*, "Book of Taharah" Ch. 22; *Sahih al-Bukhari*, "Book of Wudu" Vol. 1

[10] *Sahih al-Bukhari*, "Book on Funerals" Hadith 1253; *Sahih Muslim*, "Book in the Virtues" Hadith 4374; al-Nisa'i "Book on Funerals" Hadith 2062; *Musnad* Ahmad ibn Hanbal, Vol. 2, 269, 315, 351, and 533

stories in the books of hadith which have no harmony with the teachings of the Noble Quran.

Intercession (Shafa'ah)

The issue of Intercession (*Shafa'ah*) is one of the most controversial issues within Islam. The Shi'a school of thought and some schools within the Sunni tradition believe in the concept of Intercession, while others, like Wahabism reject it and say that whoever believes in it is not a Muslim, rather is a heretic. The Quran addresses this issue in three manners. First, there are verses which negate intercession, such as 2:123 and 2:254. Second, there are verses which say that the Intercession is exclusively the domain of Allah—He and only He has the ability to intercede, such as in 6:70 and 39:44. Third, there are verses which take precedence over the first two categories and it is in these verses that the power and ability of intercession is best defined. They state that while the Intercession is the absolute right of Allah, nevertheless, if He wishes, He can extend it to certain people among His creation. The Quran states:

> No intercessor can plead with Him except by His permission.[1]

> Who is he that can intercede with Him except with His permission?[2]

> On that Day, no intercession shall avail, except the one from whom Allah, the Most Gracious has given permission and whose word is acceptable to Him.[3]

> And they cannot intercede, except for Him with whom He is pleased.[4]

---

[1] *Noble Quran*, 10:3
[2] *Noble Quran*, 2:255
[3] *Noble Quran*, 20:109
[4] *Noble Quran*, 21:28

None shall have the power of intercession except one who has received permission or a promise from Allah, the Most Gracious.[5]

Intercession with Him profits none except for those He permits.[6]

According to these verses, certain people will have permission from Allah—such as prophets, imams, and *awliya'* (intimate friend of Allah)—to intercede and help people by the permission of Allah. Without His permission, no intercession will be accepted. Even during their lifetime, prophets had the ability to intercede on behalf of those who repented and sought forgiveness and returned to the path of Allah. The Quran states:

We sent no messenger but to be obeyed by the leave of Allah. If they who have been unjust to themselves had come to you (Prophet Muhammad) and begged Allah's forgiveness, and the Messenger had begged forgiveness for them—indeed they would have found Allah All-Forgiving, Most Merciful.[7]

(The brothers of Yusuf) said, "O our father! Ask forgiveness from Allah for our sins. Indeed, we have been sinners." He said, "I will ask my Lord for forgiveness for you." Verily, He, and only He, is the Oft-Forgiving, Most Merciful.[8]

The Prophet Muhammad has also mentioned to the people in regards to his own intercession:

---

[5] *Noble Quran*, 19:87
[6] *Noble Quran*, 34:23
[7] *Noble Quran*, 4:64
[8] *Noble Quran*, 12:97-98

I will be interceding on the Day of Judgment for whoever has faith in his heart.[9]

Each prophet before me asked Allah for something which he was granted, and I saved my request until the Day of Judgment for intercession on behalf of my nation.[10]

My intercession will be for the people who committed the cardinal sins (al-kaba'ir) except *shirk* and *dhulm* (polytheism and oppression).[11]

The Intercessors are five: the Quran, one's near relatives, trusts (amanah), your Prophet, and the family of your Prophet (the Ahlul Bayt).[12]

Shafa'ah is not to ask the prophet or the imams for protection or to ward off calamity or to bring happiness and success. Rather, it is to plead to Allah, the Almighty by the sake of those who are near to Him, like the prophets and the imams.

As the Noble Quran asserts, only those who receive promise and permission from Allah can intercede and help people on the Day of Judgment. Intercession will be for those with good intentions and good belief in this life, who neither defied Allah nor challenged His authority but, perhaps fell behind in part of their religious obligations. Their good record will help them receive the intercession of the messengers, the imams, and the believers on the Day of Judgment.

Imam Ja'far al-Sadiq, the sixth Imam of the school of Ahlul Bayt, at the time of his martyrdom called his relatives and companions

---

[9] al-Muttaqi al-Hindi, *Kanz al-Ummal,* Hadith 39043
[10] Ibid.
[11] Ibid.
[12] Ibid., Hadith 39041

and said, "Verily, our intercession will never reach one who takes the prayers lightly."[13]

---

[13] al-Majlisi, *Bihar al-Anwar*, 82:236

Calling Upon the Prophet and Imams for Help

Calling upon the Prophet and the imams (also referred to as *istighathat al-nabi wal-a'immah*) is allegorical, not literal. The Noble Quran teaches people to worship and seek help from Allah ("*iyyaka na'budu wa iyyaka nasta'in*"); however, the allegorical seeking of help is permitted in the Noble Quran. For example, in the story of Prophet Musa (Moses), "And he found there two men fighting—one from his party (*Shi'a*), and the other from his foes. The man of his own party asked him (*istighathahu*) for help against his foe, so Musa struck him with his fist and killed him."[1]

Many of the narrators of hadith narrate a prayer (*du'a*) from the Prophet which begins, "O my Lord! I turn to you by your Prophet, the Prophet of Mercy (*Allahumma, inni atawajjahu ilayka bi nabiyyika nabi al-rahma...*)." Then it says, "O Muhammad! I turn to Allah by you to solve my difficulties."[2]

It is also narrated that the feet of 'Abdullah ibn Umar al-Khattab became disabled and he could no longer walk. After being told to call upon the closest people to his heart, he said, "*Wa Muhammada!*" His feet became cured and worked properly again.[3] The Noble Quran teaches us to "seek help through patience and prayer (*sabr* and *salat*)."[4] Sabr (according to commentators of the Quran, in this context refers to fasting) and salat (prayers) are means which ultimately lead one to Allah. Thus calling upon the Prophet or Imam Ali is allegorical since all agree that Allah is the main source of support, aid, and assistance and they are just a means to Him.

---

[1] *Noble Quran,* 28:15
[2] Ibn Majah; Tirmidhi, al-Nisa'i; "*al-Husn al-Hasin*" Ibn al-Juzri
[3] al-Samhudi, *Shifa' al-Asqam*
[4] *Noble Quran,* 2:45

Some Muslims associate calling upon the Prophet or the imams as *shirk* (heresy). They argue that a person should not ask any person for help. However, we see that if a person is faced with a problem in life, often, this person will logically and naturally call upon a nearby person for help. If a person was about to drown and he called out for help, then would his seeking help from someone other than Allah make him a *mushrik* (associating one with Allah)? By the same reasoning, calling upon the Prophet or the imams is not shirk. The argument that they cannot be called upon because they are dead is also invalid, because the Quran falsifies the notion of martyrs being classified as dead, "Think not of those who are killed in the way of Allah as dead. Nay, they are alive with their Lord, and they have provision."[5] "And say not of those who are killed in the way of Allah, 'They are dead.' Nay, they are living, but you perceive it not."[6] If an ordinary Muslim was martyred (for the cause of Allah) is considered to be alive, then how can the Prophet and his family, who were not only martyrs, but whose rank also surpassed that of all other human beings, be considered dead? Calling upon the Prophet and his family does not negate the fact that Allah is the source of help and rescue in this universe. However, because these people are the closest to Him, and they enjoy a special status with Him, then calling upon them means calling upon Allah for the sake of those whom He loves.

---

[5] *Noble Quran*, 3:169
[6] *Noble Quran*, 2:154

Imam al-Mahdi

All Muslims agree that at the end of time al-Mahdi will reappear to make justice prevail on earth after being overwhelmed with injustice, corruption, and tyranny. However, the dispute between the different schools of thought is as to who he is, and whether or not he is already born. Great scholars emphasize that al-Mahdi is a member of the Ahlul Bayt (the Family of the Prophet):

> Imam al-Bukhari narrates from the Prophet Muhammad, "How will you feel once the son of Mary descends among you, and your leader (imam) is from you?"[1]

> Imam Muslim narrates from the Prophet Muhammad, "A caliph will be appearing at the end of time from my nation." Timridhi and Abu Dawud, commenting on this hadith, say that this caliph will be al-Mahdi.[2]

> Abu Dawud narrates from the Noble Prophet, "If there remained but a single day until the end of time, Allah will prolong that day until He sends a man from my progeny whose name will be like mine and who fill the earth with justice and equity as it had been filled with oppression and tyranny."[3]

> Ibn Majah narrates from the Prophet Muhammad, "We are the Ahlul Bayt for whom Allah has chosen the hereafter to this world. My Ahlul Bayt after me will face difficulties, hardships, and persecution in

---

[1] *Sahih al-Bukhari*, Vol. 4, 143
[2] *Sahih Muslim*, Vol. 2; *Sunan* Tirmidhi; *Sunan* Abu Dawud, Vol. 2, 421
[3] *Sunan* Abu Dawud, Vol. 2; 421

the land until a group of people will come from the East, bearers of black banners. They will demand the right, but it will be denied. So they will fight and emerge victorious. They will be given what they demanded but will not accept it until they give the right to rule to a man from my Ahlul Bayt, who will fill the earth with justice as it was filled with oppression."[4]

Ibn Majah also narrates from the Prophet Muhammad, "The Mahdi is from us, the Ahlul Bayt. He is among the children of Fatima."[5]

Tirmidhi narrates from the Prophet Muhammad, "A man from my Ahlul Bayt whose name is like mine will verily rule the world and if there remains but a single day before the end of time, Allah will prolong that day until he assumes rule."[6]

According to the Shi'a school of thought, Imam Muhammad ibn al-Hassan al-Mahdi was born in 255H (869AD) on the 15th of the month of Sha'ban in the city of Samarra in northern Iraq. His father was Imam Hassan al-Askari, whose lineage traces back to Imam Ali ibn Abi Talib, and his mother's name was Narjiss.

He is the last of the twelve imams for the people on earth, and with him the line of succession to the Prophet ends. Due to the necessity of having a representative from Allah present on earth, he is still, by the will of Allah, living in this world—but out of the public view. He will however reappear towards the end of human

---

[4] Ibid., Vol. 2, Hadith 4082 and 4087
[5] Ibid., Vol. 2, Hadith 4082 and 4087
[6] Tirmidhi, al-Jami'al-Sahih, Vol. 9, 74-75; For more references on this topic see: Fath al-Bari, al-Hafiz, Vol. 5. 362; Ibn Hajar al-Haythami, al-Sawa'iq Vol. 2, 212; Muntakab al-Athar, Ayatullah Lutfullah Safi, which includes over sixty hadiths from the Sunni sources and ninety hadiths from the Shi'a sources.

civilization to restore order and justice at a time when the world will be filled with evil and injustice.

Although the idea of Imam al-Mahdi still being alive after nearly thirteen centuries is difficult for some people to fathom, nonetheless, the Noble Quran sets several examples of prophets who lived even longer than al-Mahdi has lived, such as Prophet Isa, and al-Khidr (see Quran, chapter 18, verses 60-82 for his story with Prophet Musa). The Noble Quran also gives two other examples about people who died and then were resurrected by Allah. One is the example of the companions of the Cave (ashab al-kahf; see Quran, chapter 18, verse 25). The other is the example of 'Uzayr:

> Or like the one who passed by the town, and it had tumbled over its roofs. He said, 'How will Allah ever bring it alive after its death?' So Allah caused him to die for a hundred years and raised him up again. He said, 'How long did you remain dead?' He replied, 'Perhaps I remained dead a day, or part of a day.' He said, 'Nay! You have remained dead for a hundred years. Look at your food and drink. They show no change.'[7]

Furthermore, if Allah allowed Prophet Ibrahim, Prophet Musa, and Prophet Isaa to perform certain miracles, then allowing al-Mahdi to live for such an extended period of time is not difficult for Him, for He is capable of doing all things.

---

[7] Noble Quran, 2:259

Dissimulation (Taqiyyah)

Taqiyyah is the practice of hiding one's belief under duress and it is mentioned in the Noble Quran in three places:

> Let not the believers take the disbelievers as guardians instead of the believers, and whoever does this will never be helped by Allah in any way, unless you indeed fear a danger from them (*illa an tattaqu minhum tuqat*).[1]

> Whoever disbelieved in Allah after his belief—except him who is forced thereto and whose heart is at rest with faith.[2]

> And a believing man from Pharaoh's family who hid his faith....[3]

These three verses clearly point to the permissibility of concealing one's ideology and opinion whenever in danger. Those living in countries with zero tolerance for the followers of the Ahlul Bayt, where democracy is absent and tyranny, oppression, and abuse of human rights are rampant, and people are subjected to persecution, torture, and killing on account of their beliefs should according to the Quranic teachings, practice taqiyyah - to conceal their lives, wealth, properties, families, and friends. Taqiyyah should only be practiced whenever there is fear of danger or harm. If there is no fear of danger or harm, such as for the Muslims in the United States of America and Europe, then taqiyyah should not be practiced. Surah 16:106 illustrates this point, as it was revealed to allow some of the companions of the Prophet in Makkah to express

---

[1] *Noble Quran,* 3:28
[2] *Noble Quran,* 16:106
[3] *Noble Quran,* 40:28

disbelief with their tongues and hide their true faith in their hearts when they were being tortured by Abu Sufyan. Even the most prominent companion of the Prophet, 'Ammar ibn Yassir declared disbelief when the infidels were torturing him in Makkah. People came to the Prophet and complained that 'Ammar had become a disbeliever, a *kafir*. The Prophet replied, "No, indeed 'Ammar is full of faith (*iman*) from head to toe," and he told 'Ammar that if the disbelievers were to torture him again, then he should again deny his faith in public. This story is also mentioned in the explanation of verse 106 of Surah 16.

The first person in Islam to practice taqiyyah was the Messenger of Allah himself; when he concealed his mission in the beginning of Islam. For three years,[4] his mission was very secret, and in order to protect the message and the ideas he was carrying, he did not reveal them to the Quraysh until Allah commanded him to speak openly. "Therefore, proclaim openly the message of Allah— that which you are commanded—and turn away from the idolaters," as Allah instructed the Prophet.[5] Afterwards, the Prophet began openly inviting people to Islam after this period of taqiyyah. Moreover, Islamic history shows that many prominent leaders, of all schools of thought, from various recorded traditions practiced taqiyyah on different occasions. For example, Imam Abu Hanifah when he gave verdicts to abandon prayers and break fast during the month of Ramadan for the person who was being coerced. Similarly, Imam Malik was obliged to use high levels of diplomacy with the Umayyad and 'Abbasid dynasties by using Surah 3, verse 28 as justification. Imam Shafi'i also used taqiyyah in his verdict regarding a man who swore falsely by the name of Allah under coercion that he will not have to pay the *kaffarah* (expiation).[6] Imam al-Ghazzali narrates that protecting the Muslim blood is obligatory

---

[4] *Sirat* ibn Hisham, Vol. 1, 274. *Tarikh* al-Tabari, Vol. 2, 216 and 218; Ibn Sa'ad, *al-Tabaqat al-Kubra*, 200
[5] *Noble Quran*, 15:94
[6] Al-Amidi, *Difa 'an al-Kafi*, Vol. 1, 627

thus lying is obligatory, if it means preventing the shedding the blood of a Muslim.[7]

Some people associate taqiyyah with *nifaq* (hypocrisy). However, hypocrisy is defined as falsely displaying faith (*iman*) while hiding disbelief (*kufr*), whereas taqiyyah is showing agreement, while in the heart there is disagreement in order to protect one's self, family, money, or religion.

---

[7] al-Ghazzali, *Ihya 'Ulum al-Din*

Seeing Allah (Ru'yat Allah)

The Shi'a school of thought absolutely denies what others say that Allah can be seen since He has no image or body. However, other schools of thought accept several hadiths that not only claim that Allah has physical parts; but also that He will be seen on the Day of Judgment like any other objects are seen. They also claim that Allah occupies space and travels from one place to another. The basis for these arguments are hadiths and not the Noble Quran. We mention some of these narrations:

> Our Lord, before creating His creation, did not have anything with Him, underneath Him was air, above Him was air, then he created His throne on water.[1]

> (On the Day of Judgment) It will be said to Hell, 'Are you filled up?' It will say, 'Are there any more?' So the Lord, Blessed and Exalted is He will put His leg into it, whereupon it will say, 'Now I am full!'[2]

> We were sitting with the Messenger of Allah when he looked at the full moon and observed, 'You shall see your Lord as you are seeing this moon, and you will not be harmed by seeing Him.'[3]

---

[1] *Sunan* ibn Majah, "Introduction"; *Sunan* al-Tirmidhi, "Explanations of Surah Hud"; *Musnad* Ahmad ibn Hanbal. Vol. 4, 11-12

[2] *Sahih al-Bukhari*, Vol. 3, 128, Vol. 4, 191, Vol. 4, 129 of Anas. Some narrations say: "foot" instead of "leg."

[3] *Sahih al-Bukhari*, "Book on the Times of Prayers" Hadith 521 and 539, Vol. 10. 18 and 20, "Interpretation of the Noble Quran," Hadith 4473, "Monotheism" Hadith 6882-6884; *Sahih Muslim*, "Book on masjids and Places of Performing Prayers" Hadith 1002; *Tirmidhi*, "Book on the Description of Paradise" Hadith 2474; Abu Dawud, Book on the Sunnah,

The last narration, in particular, asserts that people will see Allah with their physical eyes, regardless of whether they are among the good or among the hypocrites. Seeing Allah means that Allah must have a physical body and occupy physical space. Imam Malik ibn Anas and Imam al-Shafi'i accept this opinion, and Imam Ahmad ibn Hanbal considers this belief among the fundamentals of the religion.

The opinion of the followers of the Ahlul Bayt is that seeing Allah is impossible. This view is supported by the Noble Quran and logic. The Noble Quran says clearly, "No vision can grasp Him, but His grasp is over all vision."[4] Furthermore, there are multiple examples of people asking to see Allah and the response of Allah, the Exalted was:

> And remember when you said, 'O people of Musa, We shall never believe in you until we see Allah plainly.' But you were seized with a thunderbolt while you were looking. Then We raised you up after death so that you might be grateful.[5]

> The People of the Scripture ask you (O Muhammad) to cause a book to descend upon them from Heaven. Indeed, they asked Musa for even greater than that when they said, 'Show us Allah in public,' but they were struck with thunder and lightening for their wickedness. [6]

> And those who expect not a meeting with Us say, 'Why are not the angels sent down to us?' or 'Why do we not see our Lord?' Indeed, they think too

---

Hadith 4104; Ibn Majah, "Book on the Introduction" Hadith 173; *Musnad Ahmad ibn Hanbal,* Vol. 4. 360, 362, and 365

[4] *Noble Quran,* 6:102
[5] *Noble Quran,* 2:55
[6] *Noble Quran,* 4:53

highly of themselves and are scornful with great pride.[7]

When Musa came to the place appointed by Us, and his Lord addressed him, he said, 'O Lord! Show Yourself to me so that I may look upon You.' Allah said, 'By no means can you see Me, but look at the mountain—if it abides in its place then you shall see Me.' When his Lord manifested His glory to the mountain, He made it like dust, and Musa fell in a swoon. When he recovered his senses, he said, 'Glory be to You. To You do I turn in repentance and I am the first to believe.'[8]

If seeing Allah was impossible for the prophets and the messengers of Allah then it is clearly impossible for all other people as well; whether during this life or in the Hereafter.

Logically speaking, in order to see an object, the object must have several qualities. First, it must have a specific direction, such as in front of or to the left or right of the observer. Second, a distance must exist between the one seeing and the thing being seen. Seeing would be impossible if the distance became longer or shorter. Allah the Almighty is not a physical object that we can pin-point and ultimately see, nor does He occupy space. Although the Noble Quran says, "He is the Supreme, watching over His worshippers,"[9] and "They revere their Lord high above them"[10]—"above them"—refers to the Almighty being above His servants in His might, power, and loftiness - not in place, space, area, elevation, or physical location. Such qualities do not apply to Him. During his ascension to Heaven, the Prophet called upon his Lord by the words, "You are as You have praised Your Own Self." While Prophet Yunus called upon his Lord from the bottom of the sea saying, "There is no God but You! Glory

---

[7] *Noble Quran*, 25:21
[8] *Noble Quran*, 7:143
[9] *Noble Quran*, 6:61
[10] *Noble Quran*, 16:50

be to You!"[11] Regarding Prophet Yunus, the Prophet Muhammad said, "Do not exalt me over him in nearness to Allah just because I reached the high throne, whereas he was in the bottom of the sea, because the adored One is above being confined to a space or direction."

Imam Ali was asked by one of his companions, Tha'lab al-Yamani whether he had seen his Lord. Imam Ali replied, "How can I worship something that I do not see?" When asked how he saw Him, Imam Ali replied, "Eyes do not reach Him with physical sight, but the hearts reach Him with the realities of belief."[12] There are many things which people cannot reach and have no physical access to but which people still believe in. Imam Ja'far al-Sadiq, the sixth Imam, was once asked, "will Allah be seen on the Day of Resurrection?" His answer was, "May He be exalted and glorified from that! The eyes can only reach an object which has color and shape, but Allah, the Exalted, is the Creator of colors and shapes."

Similar aspects of Allah, such as His "hand" or His "face" are referred to as allegorically. The "Hand of Allah" refers to His power and might, and "His Face" refers to different things. The first step in the Oneness and Monotheism of Allah is the understanding that Allah is not a body and will never be seen and that He is unique, as the Noble Quran states, "There is nothing like Him."[13]

---

[11] *Noble Quran*, 21:87
[12] *Nahj al-Balagha*
[13] *Noble Quran*, 42:11

The Prayers Upon the Prophet
(Salat 'ala an-Nabi)

Muslims are commanded by the Noble Quran (33:56) to send their prayers upon the Prophet Muhammad in which Allah has said:

> 'Indeed God and His angels bless the Prophet; O you who have faith! Invoke blessings on him and invoke Peace upon him in a worthy manner.'

The Prophet indicated how to do this and also commanded his followers not to send their prayers only upon himself, but always to send their prayers simultaneously upon his family as well. He is quoted to have said:

> 'Do not send me an amputated prayer.' The companions asked, 'What is an amputated prayer?' He said, 'When you say, 'Allahumma, salli 'ala Muhammad' and stop. Rather, you should say, 'Allahumma, salli 'ala Muhammad wa al-e-Muhammad.'[1]

> The supplication will be intercepted (not accepted) until it is prayed upon the Prophet and his family.[2]

> On the authority of 'Abdullah ibn Abi Layla, as reported by Imam al-Bukhari, the Messenger of Allah came to us and we said to him, 'We have learned how to invoke peace upon you; how should we pray for you?' He (the Prophet) said, 'Say: O Allah, bless Muhammad and his family as You blessed the family of Ibrahim. Verily, You are the

---

[1] *Yanabi' al-Muwaddah*, Vol. 2, 59; Ibn Hajar, *al-Sawa'iq al-Muhriqah*, Ch. 11. Sect. 1

[2] *Yanabi' al-Muwaddah*, Vol. 2, 59

Praiseworthy, the Glorious. Grant favor to Muhammad and the members of his household as You granted favor to the members of the household of Ibrahim in the world. Verily, You are the Praiseworthy, the Glorious.'[3]

When teaching his companions the *salat* (prayer), the Prophet specifically included his progeny (*al-e-Muhammad*). Hence, Muslims must adhere to the teachings of the Prophet and send blessings upon all of those whom he commanded for us to do.

---

[3] *Sahih al-Bukhari*, "Book on Traditions of Prophets" Hadith 3119, "Interpretation of the Noble Quran" Hadith 4423, "Supplication" Hadith 5880; *Sahih Muslim*, "Book on Prayer" Hadith 614; al-Tirmidhi, "Book on Prayer" Hadith 445; al-Nisa'i, "Book on Inattention" Hadith 1270-1272; Abu Dawud, "Book on Prayer" Hadith 830; Ibn Majah, "Book on Immediate Call for Prayer" Hadith 894; *Musnad* Ahmad ibn Hanbal, Vol. 4, 241, 243, and 244; al-Darami, "Book on Prayer" Hadith 1308

Issues Pertaining to the
Practice of the Prayers

Wiping the Feet During Ablution (Wudu)

The followers of the Ahlul Bayt comply by what the Noble Quran teaches them to do during *wudu* (ablution) in regards to wiping their feet, rather than washing them. The Noble Quran commands, "O you who believe! When you intend (to perform) your prayers, wash your faces and your hands from the elbows and wipe (by passing wet hands over) your head and your feet up to the ankles."[1] Those who practice the washing of their feet during wudu argue that "your feet" in the Noble Quran is linked to washing the face, whereas the followers of the Ahlul Bayt argue that "your feet" is linked to rubbing the head; therefore, it should be wiped, and not washed.

In support of the latter view, Ibn 'Abbas narrates from the Prophet, that they used to rub their feet during the time of the Prophet.[2] Undoubtedly, all Muslims at the time of the Holy Messenger of Allah used to perform wudu in the same way. No disagreements occurred between them since the Messenger of Allah was present among them and all the Muslims used to submit their disagreements to him in accordance with the Noble Quran, "And if you differ in anything amongst yourselves, refer it to Allah and His Messenger."[3] The same situation existed during the time of the first caliph, Abu Bakr (11-13H) and no disagreements over the performance of wudu have been reported from that time period either. Similar was the period of the second caliph, 'Umar ibn al-

---

[1] *Noble Quran,* 5:6
[2] al-Shahrastani, *Wudhu' al-Nabi*
[3] *Noble Quran,* 4:59

Khattab (13-23H), except for the fact, that he allowed wiping of the socks rather than the bare feet as the Noble Quran directs (5:6). However, the disagreement regarding the performance of the wudu began during the time of the third caliph, 'Uthman ibn Affan (23-35H) when he began to wash his feet instead of wiping them.[4] Al-Muttaqi al-Hindi, in his book *Kanz al-'Ummal*[5] mentions that the third caliph, 'Uthman ibn Affan (during his caliphate) was the first to differ in performing the wudu. In *Sahih al-Muslim*[6] and *Kanz al-'Ummal*,[7] 'Uthman ibn Affan says that during his caliphate, some of the companions of the Prophet who performed their wudu differently than himself attributed their practice to the Prophet. More than twenty narrations—all narrated by the third caliph—are about his new manner of performing wudu. These traditions indicate his establishment of the new method.

Some prominent Muslim historians, such as Ibn Abi al-Hadid al-Mu'tazili[8] regard this trend as nothing new in the tradition of the third caliph since he was known for his numerous innovations (into the faith of Islam). There is a near consensus among the Muslim historians that the third caliph, 'Uthman was murdered by Muslim revolutionaries in 35H. because of political and financial issues. However, other Muslim historians interpret the third caliph's introductions (regarding some of the religious rules during the last six years of his caliphate) as a departure from the tradition of the first and second caliphs. The majority of the Muslims during his caliphate looked at the third caliph as a follower of the first and second caliphs, and the implementer of their practices. Since the third caliph witnessed numerous introductions during the time of the second caliph, and saw himself religiously and intellectually no less than his predecessors[9], thus he decided to depart from the

---

[4] *Sahih al-Bukhari*, Vol. 1, 52; *Sahih Muslim*, Vol. 1, 204
[5] al-Muttaqi al-Hindi, *Kanz al-'Ummal*, Hadith 26890, Vol. 9, 443
[6] *Sahih Muslim* Vol. 1, 207-208
[7] al-Muttaqi al-Hindi, *Kanz al-'Ummal*, Hadith 26797, Vol. 9, 423
[8] Ibn Abi al-Hadid, *Sharh Nahj al-Balagha*, Vol. 1, 199-200
[9] al-Tabari, *Tarikh*, Vol. 4, 339

previous policy and have an independent opinion regarding different political, financial, and jurisprudential issues such as, washing the feet during wudu.

Although some people today consider washing the feet to lead to better cleanliness and hygiene than merely wiping the feet; however, Allah the Almighty who legislated all the acts of worship, including the wudu, is more aware of the advantages and disadvantages of washing or wiping the feet. It has been narrated that Imam Ali ibn Abi Talib said, "If religion was according to human opinion, the bottom of the foot would be more worthy of wiping than the top. But I saw the Messenger of Allah wiping the top of his feet."[10]

Combining the Prayers

All Muslims agree that there are five mandatory prayers throughout the day and night. They also agree that these five daily prayers have specific times in which they must be performed, and that combining the prayers is, at least, sometimes permissible (saying the *dhuhr* (noon) prayer then immediately followed by the *asr* (afternoon) prayer, or saying the *maghrib* (post-sunset) prayer immediately followed by the *isha* (night) prayer). The Maliki, Shafi'i, and Hanbali schools of thought agree that combining of the prayers while traveling is permitted, but they do not allow combining of the prayers for other reasons. The Hanafi school of thought permits combining of the prayers only on the day of Arafat. Whereas the *Imami* Shi'a school of thought, allows combining of the prayers in all cases—while traveling or not, for any other reason, during war and peace, while the weather is rainy or not, and so on. The real dispute is as to *when* the exact beginning and end of the prayer times are. Thus, the dispute must be referred to the Noble Quran and narrations of the Prophet Muhammad.

---

[10] Abu Shaybah, *al-Musannatf*, Hadith 6, Vol. 1, 30; *Sunan* Abi Dawud, Hadith 164, Vol. 1, 42

Three verses in the Noble Quran speak of the times for the prayers. Allah, the Exalted says, "Perform the prayers from mid-day until the darkness of the night, and recite the Quran in the early dawn. Verily, the recitation of the Quran in the early dawn is ever-witnessed."[11] "Mid-day" refers to the shared time for the dhuhr and asr prayers, "the darkness of the night" refers to the shared time of the mahrib and isha prayers, and "early dawn" refers to the *fajr* (dawn) prayer. The Noble Quran clearly and simply states that there are three main times for the five daily prayers. Although the prayers are five, they fall into three main periods of time. The great Sunni scholar, Fakhr al-Din al-Razi understood this interpretation from this verse also.[12] Of course, the prayers must be done in order; the dhuhr prayer must be performed before the asr prayer, and the maghrib prayer must be performed before the isha prayer.

The Noble Quran also says, "And perform the prayers at the two ends of the day, and in some hours of the night. Verily, the good deeds remove the evil deeds. That is a reminder for the mindful."[13] Muslim jurists and Quran commentators agree that this verse refers to the five compulsory prayers, as the Noble Quran states, it determines the timing of the prayers—the three main times; two of them at the "ends of the day" and the third in "some hours of the night." The first, "ends of the day" is the time of the morning prayer, the second, "ends of the day" begins at noon and ends at sunset (making this the time for the dhuhr and asr prayers), and the "hours of the night" is the third main time in which the maghrib and isha prayers should be recited; these prayers extend from the beginning of the night until midnight.

A similar division of times is expressed in a third verse, "So bear with patience (O Muhammad) all that they say, and glorify the praises of your Lord before the rising of the sun, and before its setting, and during a part of the night, also glorify His praises, and

---

[11] *Noble Quran,* 17:78
[12] Fakhr al-Din al-Razi, *Tafsir,* Vol. 5, 428
[13] *Noble Quran,*11:114

so likewise after the prostrations."[14] As in the previous verse, the jurists and the commentators also agree that this verse refers to the times of the five mandatory prayers; in addition to dividing the time for the prayers into three segments: first, the time from dawn until sunrise which is the time for the dawn prayers (fajr); second, the time from noon until sunset, which is the time for the noon and afternoon prayers; and third, the "part of the night" which extends from after sunset until midnight, which is the time for the evening and night prayers. Referring to the last part of the cited verse (50:39-40), "And so likewise after the prostration," according to the commentators, refers either to the nawafil (recommended) prayers, or specifically to salat al-layl (the midnight prayer) which are among the highly recommended prayers.

Imam al-Bukhari and others report that the Prophet used to combine his prayers into three sections of time, "The Messenger of Allah observed the noon and afternoon prayers together and the sunset and night prayers together without being in a state of fear or while on a journey."[15] Imam Muslim narrates the same hadith and adds that when the Prophet was asked by Ibn al-'Abbas why he authorized combining the two prayers, the Prophet replied that he did not want to cause difficulty for his nation.[16] In the same book, Ibn al-'Abbas himself narrates that they used to combine the two prayers during the time of the Prophet.[17] Therefore, both the Noble Quran and the tradition of the Prophet indicate clear authorization and permission to combine the two prayers without any particular

---

[14] *Noble Quran*, 50:39-40

[15] *Sahih al-Bukhari*, "Book on Times of Prayers" Hadith 510 and 529, "Book on Friday Prayer" Hadith 1103; *Sahih Muslim*, "Book on the Prayer of Travellers" Hadith 1146; al-Tirmidhi, "Book on Prayer" Hadith 172; al-Nisa'i, "Book on Timings" Hadith 585, 597-599; Abu Dawud, "Book on Prayer" Hadith 1024, 1025, and 1027; *Musnad* Ahmad ibn Hanbal, Vol. 1:217, 221, 223, 251, 273, 283, 285, 346, 349, 351, 354, 360, and 366; Malik, "Book on Shortening the Prayer while Travelling" Hadith 300

[16] *Sahih Muslim*, "Book of the Prayers of Travellers" Ch. 6, Hadith 50-54

[17] *Sahih Muslim*, Ch. 6-8, Hadith 58-62

reason. It also asserts that Allah the Merciful made His religion easy for the believers.

The Adhan (Call to Prayer); "Hayya 'ala Khayril 'Amal" (Come to the Best of Deeds)

The entire *adhan* (call to prayer) was taught to the Prophet Muhammad by Allah on the night he ascended to Heaven, and the prayers were made obligatory on him that same night.[18] The original adhan taught to him contained the phrase "*hayya 'ala khayril 'amal*" (come to the best of deeds); however, at the time the Islamic state was expanding, the second caliph, 'Umar ibn al-Khattab thought that this phrase would discourage people from performing *jihad* (defense fighting) and thus ordered it to be removed from the adhan. Imam Muslim narrates, on the authority of Ibn Mas'ud that the Prophet had commanded the Muslims to say in the adhan and *iqaama* (the call that signals the beginning of the prayer) "*hayya 'ala khayril 'amal*," but once 'Umar assumed authority he dropped that phrase.[19] He also says that Ali ibn Abi Talib and his followers, as well as, 'Abdullah, the son of 'Umar did not drop this phrase.[20]

'Umar ibn al-Khattab has been narrated to have said, "O people, three things existed during the time of the Messenger of Allah that I prohibit and make unlawful and will punish for, they are: *mut'at al-hajj, mut'at al-nisa,* and *'hayya 'ala khayr al-'amal.'* (the Mut'ah of the Hajj, mut'ah of the woman and 'hasten towards the best of deeds')"[21]

Malik ibn Anas narrates the story of how *'hayya 'ala khayr al-'amal'* (Hasten towards the best of deeds) was replaced by "*al-salat khayrun min al-nawm*" (The prayers are better than sleep.) Anas said, "The *mu'adhdhin* (the person making the call to prayer) came to 'Umar ibn al-Khattab to announce the morning prayers and found

---

[18] al-Muttaqi al-Hindi, *Kanz al-Ummal*, Hadith 397, Vol. 6; al-Hakim, *al-Mustadrak*, Vol. 3; 1

[19] *Sahih Muslim*, Vol. 1, 48

[20] al-Sirah *al-Halabiyyah*, Vol. 4, 56

[21] *Sharh al-Tajrid; Musnad* Ahmad ibn Hanbal, Vol. 1, 49

him asleep, so he said to him, '*al-salat khayrun min al-nawm*' (prayer is better than sleep). 'Umar liked this sentence very much, so he ordered that it be included in the adhan for the morning prayers."[22] Imam Muslim and Abu Dawud also concur that this sentence was not part of the adhan during the time of the Prophet, and Tirmidhi asserts that 'Umar was the one who added it.[23]

Some people may wonder why the Shi'a, in the adhan, include: "*Ashhadu anna Ali`yan waliuAllah*" ("I testify that Ali is the close friend of Allah") after the first two testimonies. All the Shi'a jurists and scholars have a consensus that this sentence is not an obligatory part of the adhan; nonetheless, saying it is a tradition. However, if anyone says it in the adhan, believing it to be obligatory, then his or her adhan will become void. The Shi'as believe it began during the time of the Prophet, on the day of Ghadir after he appointed Imam Ali as his successor, during which the Muslims paid their allegiance to Imam Ali, and Abu Dharr al-Ghifari recited the adhan and added the phrase: "*Ashhadu anna Ali`yan wali Allah.*" Afterwards, the Muslims came to the Prophet and said that they had heard something new in the adhan. When the Prophet asked what they had heard, they replied, we heard the phrase, "*Ashhadu anna 'Aliyan wali Allah*" in the adhan. The Prophet asked them whether they had not just acknowledged this same phrase to Imam Ali when they gave their allegiance (*bay'ah*) to him.

Crossing the Hands in Prayer (Takfir[24])

The Messenger of Allah has said, "Perform your prayers as you see me performing my prayers." Therefore, crossing the hands makes the prayers void in the *Imamiyyah* (those who believe in the 12 imams who succeeded the Noble Prophet as appointed by Allah)

---

[22] Malik ibn Anas, *Kitab al-Muwatta'*, Ch. "Adhan"

[23] *Sunan* al-Tirmidhi, Vol. 1, 64

[24] *Takfir* comes from the Arabic word for "covering," and since crossing the hands covers part of the chest it is called *takfir*.

school of thought, since it is deemed as the habit of the Magians[25] (*Majus*).[26] However, in the Hanafi and Shafi'i schools, it is recommended (*mustahhab*) to cross the hands. Nevertheless, the two schools differ slightly in the hand posture; the Shafi'i school says to cross the right hand on top of the left above the belly, while the Hanafi says to hold the hands below the belly.

Concluding the Prayers with Three Takbirs (Saying: Allahu Akbar!)

The Messenger of Allah used to conclude his prayers with three *takbirs*. Imam Muslim narrates this fact on the authority of Ibn al-'Abbas who says, "We knew that the Prophet had concluded his prayers when he would recit the three takbirats."[27]

Prostrating on Earth (Turbah)

Prostrating on the earth (*turbah*) or nature made material does not in any way imply worshipping the earth or stone which one is prostrating upon. As a practice, it has a firm foundation in the tradition of the Prophet, which the Noble Quran teaches the Muslims to follow in all aspects.

Imam al-Bukhari narrates that the Prophet said, "I have been given five things which were not granted to anyone (any other prophet) before me:

1. Every apostle was sent particularly to his own people, whereas I have been sent to all people - red and yellow.

2. The spoils of war have been made lawful for me, and these were never made lawful for anyone before me.

---

[25] Magians are people who consider fire as the purest and noblest element, and worship it as an emblem of Allah. They are mentioned in the *Noble Quran*, 22:17

[26] al-Kulayni, *al-Kafi*, Vol. 3, 336; al-Tusi, *al-Ta'dhib*, Vol. 2, 84 and 309

[27] *Sahih Muslim*, Vol. 1, 219

3. The earth has been made pure and a place of prostration for me, so whenever the time of prayer comes for any one of you, he should pray wherever he is (upon the ground).

4. I have been supported by awe (to cause fear and intimidation to enter the hearts of the Prophet's enemies) from the distance (which if covered, would take one month to cross).

5. I have been granted intercession.[28]

In regards to the subject, the third narration very clearly states that the earth (the dust and the stones) is a place of prostration. In the history of Islam, the Prophet Muhammad has shown that his masjid in Madina had no floor covering; it was only dust, although numerous types of rugs and furnishings existed at that time. Since this masjid did not have a carpet or any other type of floor covering thus when it rained the floor of the masjid would turn into mud; but still, the Muslims prostrated on the mud and did not put any carpets or rugs down. Many other narrations are as follows:

> Abu Sa'id al-Khidri, a companion of the Prophet reported, "I saw with my own eyes, the Messenger of Allah had on his nose the traces of rain and mud."

> Imam al-Bukhari narrates that when the Prophet used to do the prayers in his own room, he would pray on *khumra* (a solid piece of dirt or a piece of straw).

---

[28] *Sahih al-Bukhari*, "Book on Making Ablutions with Sand or Earth" Hadith 323, "Prayer", Hadith 419, "The Prescribed Fifth Portion" Hadith 2890; *Sahih Muslim*, "Book on masjids and Places of Performing Prayers," Hadith 810; al-Nisa'i, "Book on Washing and the Dry Ablution", Hadith 429, "masjids" Hadith 728; *Musnad* Ahmad ibn Hanbal, Vol. 3, 305; al-Darami, "Book on Prayer", Hadith 1353

> The Messenger of Allah performed his prayer and I (one of the wives of the Prophet) was lying down opposite to him while I was in menses. Sometimes his clothes touched me when he prostrated, and he used to prostrate on *khumra*.[29]

> One of the wives of the Prophet said, "I never saw the Prophet (while prostrating) prevent his face from touching the earth."[30]

> Wa'il, one of the Prophet's companions narrates, "I saw (that) the Prophet, once he prostrated touched his forehead and nose on the earth."[31]

Other narrations say that the Prophet prohibited the Muslims from prostrating on materials other than the earth. One day he saw a man prostrating on some cloth from his turban. The Prophet pointed to him and told him to remove his turban and to touch his actual forehead on the ground.[32]

Despite the immense heat of the ground, the Prophet and his companions used to prostrate on it. A great companion of the Prophet, Jabir ibn 'Abdullah al-Ansari says, "I used to pray the noon prayers with the Messenger of Allah and I used to take a bunch of

---

[29] *Sahih al-Bukhari*, "Book on Menstruation", Hadith 321, "Book on Prayer," Hadith 366, 487, and 488; *Sahih Muslim*, "Book on Prayer", Hadith 797; al-Nisa'i, "Book on masjids", Hadith 730; Abu Dawud, "Book on Prayer", Hadith 560; Ibn Majah, "Book on Immediate Call for Prayer", Hadith 1018; *Musnad* Ahmad ibn Hanbal, Vol. 6, 330, 331, 335, and 336; al-Darami, "Book on Prayer" Hadith 1338

[30] *Musnad* Ahmad ibn Hanbal, Vol. 6, 58; al-Muttaqi al-Hindi, *Kanz al-Ummal*, Vol. 4, 212

[31] al-Jassas, *Ahkam al-Quran*, Vol. 3, 36; *Musnad* Ahmad ibn Hanbal, Vol. 4, 315

[32] al-Hiythami, *Sunan al-Bayhaqi*, Vol. 2, 105; Ibn Hajar, *al-Isabah li Ma'rifat al-Sahabah*, Vol. 2, 201

pebbles in my palm to cool them because of the enormous heat so I could prostrate on them."[33]

Another companion of the Prophet, Anas ibn Malik narrates, "We used to pray with the Messenger of Allah during the enormous heat, and one of us would take pebbles in our hands and once they were cool, put them down and prostrate on them."[34]

Al-Khabbab ibn al-Arth, another companion of the Prophet says, "We complained to the Messenger of Allah about the intensity of the heat of the ground and its effects on our foreheads and palms (during prostration) but the Prophet did not excuse us from praying on the ground."[35]

Abu Ubaidah, also a companion of the Prophet narrates that the companion ibn Mas'ud never prostrated (on anything) except on the earth,[36] while the companion 'Ibada ibn al-Samit has been narrated to have pushed back his turban to allow his forehead to touch the ground.[37]

During the times of the first, second, third, and fourth caliphs the Muslims used to prostrate on the dust. Abu Umayyah narrates that the first caliph, Abu Bakr used to prostrate and pray on the earth.[38] Prostrating on the earth was also the habit of the *tabi'in* (those who did not see the Prophet but met his companions). Masruq ibn al-Ajda', a prominent tabi'in and a faithful jurist, and a student of 'Abdullah ibn Mas'ud made for himself a tablet from the

---

[33] *Sahih* al-Nisa'i, Vol. 2, 204; al-Hiythami, *Sunan* al-Bayhaqi, Vol. 1, 439;/ *Musnad* Ahmad ibn Hanbal, Vol. 3, 327

[34] al-Hiythami, *Sunan* al-Bayhaqi, Vol. 2, 105; *Nayl al-Awtar*, Vol. 2, 268

[35] al-Hiythami, *Sunan* al-Bayhaqi, Vol. 2, 106

[36] *Majma 'al-Zawa'id*, Vol. 2, 57

[37] al-Hiythami, *Sunan* al-Bayhaqi; *Sunan al-Kubra*. Vol. 2, 105

[38] al-Muttaqi al-Hindi, *Kanz al-Ummal*; al-Hiythami, *Sunan* al-Bayhaqi; *Sunan al-Kubra*, Vol. 4, 212, Vol. 2

dirt of Madina and used it to prostrate on, taking it with him on his trips, especially when he boarded ships.[39]

The people closest to the Prophet, the Ahlul Bayt were also very firm in their practice of prostrating on the earth, and in doing so, were following the tradition of their grandfather, the Messenger of Allah. Imam Ja'far al-Sadiq, the sixth Imam said, "Prostration is not permitted except on the earth and whatever grows from it except on those things that are eaten or made of cotton."[40] When he was asked whether having one's turban touch the earth instead of the forehead was acceptable, he replied that this was not sufficient unless the forehead actually touched the earth.[41] His companion and student, Hisham ibn al-Hakam asked him whether all seven positions (forehead, hands, knees, and big toes) needed to touch the earth during prostration, Imam al-Sadiq replied that as long as the forehead touched the earth, there was no need for the other six areas to touch the earth. Thus, people can use carpets or prayer rugs to pray on as long as the forehead itself touches the earth. However, prostrating by putting the forehead on a piece of cloth, carpet, nylon, sheet, wool, or anything that is not a product of the earth (excluding items which are eaten or worn; things upon which prostration is not permissible) would not be considered prostrating on the earth.

Apart from the issue of validity of prostration, prostrating on the earth has very significant indications and lessons for a believer. Prostrating itself is a gesture of humiliation and insignificance before the Almighty, and if it is done on the dirt then it will have more effect than prostrating on a carpet. The Messenger of Allah said, "Make your faces dusty and cover your noses with dust."[42] When Imam Ja'far al-Sadiq was asked about the philosophy behind prostrating on the earth, he replied, "Prostration is surrendering

---

[39] Ibn Sa'ad, *al-Tabaqat al-Kubra*, Vol. 6, 53
[40] *Wasa'il al-Shi'ah*, Vol. 3, 592
[41] Ibid.
[42] *al-Targhib wal-Tarhib*, Vol. 1, 581

and humiliation to the Almighty. Therefore, it shouldn't be on that which is worn and eaten because people are slaves of what they eat and wear, and prostration is the worshipping of Allah, so one should not put his forehead during prostration on that which is worshipped by the people (food and clothing) and that which conceits people."[43]

Of course, every rule has its exception. Certain narrations allow people in times of emergency, such as imprisonment or being in a place (e.g., a ship or an airplane) in which neither earth nor a piece of wood, leaf, or paper is available to prostrate on. Therefore, in these cases, people can prostrate either on the hem of their clothing or on carpet, for the Messenger of Allah has said, "Nothing has been forbidden to man, except that Allah permits it for whoever is **compelled** (in times of emergency)."

Why Pray on the Soil of Karbala?

The followers of Ahlul Bayt prefer to prostrate on the earth of Karbala, where the great martyrs are buried and which holds the memory of the great sacrifice of Imam Husayn, grandson of the Prophet. They do not cherish the physical soil so much as the principles of Imam Husayn and his great revolution which saved Islam from corruption, deterioration, and the tyranny of the wrongdoers. Many imams from the school of Ahlul Bayt have narrated that prostrating on the soil of Karbala penetrates the seven veils separating the person praying from Allah, the Exalted.

Conventional wisdom also determines that some lands are better than others. This fact is normal and rational, and has been agreed upon by many nations, governments, authorities, and religions. Such is the case with places and buildings related to Almighty Allah. They enjoy a special status whose injunctions, rights, and obligations are sanctioned and safeguarded. For example, the Ka'bah has an injunction of its own, as does the Masjid of the Prophet in Madina.

---

[43] *Wasa'il al-Shi'ah*, Vol. 3, 591

The land of Karbala is similar, for the Prophet has been recorded to have taken the soil from it, smelled it, and kissed it. The wife of the Prophet, Um Salamah also carried a piece of the soil of Karbala in her clothes. The Messenger of Allah has been narrated to have told Um Salamah, "Jibrail has come to me and informed me that some of my nation will assassinate my son Husayn in Iraq, and he brought me a piece of that soil." He gave that piece of soil to his wife and said, "When it turns into fresh blood, then know that my son Husayn has been murdered." Um Salamah took the soil and put it in a bottle. When Imam Husayn left for Iraq in 61H, she checked the bottle every day. One day, on the 10th of Muharram, she came to the bottle and saw that the dust had turned into fresh blood, and started screaming. The women of Bani Hashim gathered around her and asked what was wrong; she told them that Husayn had been killed. When they asked her how she knew this, she narrated the story, and they joined her in lamentation and crying for Imam Husayn.[44]

Hisham ibn Muhammad has said, "When water was released to overwhelm and obliterate the grave of Husayn, it dried after forty days, and the grave was completely left without any trace. A Bedouin from Bani Asad came and sampled the soil, one handful after another, smelling it each time, until he was able to identify the grave of Husayn, whereupon he wept and said, "May my parents be sacrificed for you! How sweet you smelled when you were alive, and how sweet your soil smells even when you are dead!" Then he wept again and composed this poem, "Out of enmity they wanted to obliterate his grave, but the good smell of the soil led to the grave."[45]

---

[44] al-Suyuti al-Shafi'i, *al-Khasa'is*, Vol. 2, 125; al-Maghazali, *al-Manaqib*, 313; *Musnad* Ahmad ibn Hanbal, Vol. 6, 294; al-Dimishqi, *Tarikh al-Islam*, Vol. 3, 11; *al-Bidayah wal-Nihayah*, Vol. 6, 230; Ibn 'Abd Rabbah, *al-'Aqd al-Farid*, Vol. 2, 219; al-Muttaqi al-Hindi, *Kanz al-Ummal*, Vol. 5, 110

[45] *Tarikh ibn Asakir*, Vol. 4, 342; Hafiz al-Kanji, *al-Kifayah*, 293

The first to prostrate on the soil of Karbala (where Imam Husayn was beheaded and buried) was his son, Ali ibn al-Husayn Zayn al-Abidin, the fourth Imam of the school of Ahlul Bayt, the great-grandson of the Messenger of Allah. Immediately after he buried his father in Karbala, he took a handful of the soil, made the earth into a solid piece and used it to prostrate upon. After him, his son Imam Muhammad al-Baqir and his grandson, Imam Ja'far al-Sadiq did the same. Imam Zayn al-Abidin and Imam al-Sadiq made prayer beads from the burial dust of Imam Husayn, and Imam al-Sadiq narrates that the daughter of the Messenger of Allah, Lady Fatima al-Zahra used to carry prayer beads made from twisted wooden threads with which she would praise and glorify Allah, the Exalted. But after Hamzah ibn 'Abdul Muttalib was killed in the Battle of Uhud, she took the soil from his grave and made prayer beads from it and used them to glorify Allah. People learned her habit and did the same when Imam Husayn was martyred; taking the soil of his grave and using it to make prayer beads.

Prayers for the Dead (Salat al-Mayyit)

During the time of the Prophet, the prayers over the newly deceased had five *takbirs* (units). Ahmad ibn Hanbal narrates from 'Abd al-A'la, "I prayed behind Zayd ibn Arqam over a dead body, and I did the takbirat five times." A man stood behind him and held his hand and asked whether he had forgotten. 'Abd al-A'la replied, "No, but I prayed behind Abul-Qasim Muhammad and he did five takbirat, and I would not do other than that."[46]

For reference, al-Suyuti mentions the name of the companion who changed the number of takbirs from five to four.[47]

Tarawih Prayers

Imam al-Bukhari narrates from 'Abdullah ibn 'Abd al-Qari, "In one of the nights of the month of Ramadan, I went to the masjid

---

[46] *Musnad* Ahmad ibn Hanbal, Vol. 4, 370; *Sahih Muslim*, "Prayers over the Graves"; *Sahih al-Nisa'i*, "Kitab al-Janazah"

[47] al-Suyuti, *al-Kamil*, Vol. 15, 29; al-Suyuti, *Tarikh al-Khulafa'*, 137

with 'Umar ibn al-Khattab. We saw the people in scattered groups, with individuals praying by themselves. Others were praying with a group praying behind them. 'Umar looked at me and said, 'In my opinion, if I can bring all these people together behind one who recites, then it would be better.' So, he gathered them and made 'Ubay ibn Ka'ab lead them in prayers. I went with him another night to the masjid, and saw people all praying together behind a person reciting. 'Umar looked at them and said, '*Ni'mat al-bid'ah hadhihi* ('This is a good innovation').'"[48]

In the Shi'a tradition, the recommended prayers (*al-nawafil*) during the month of Ramadan are performed individually.

---

[48] *Sahih al-Bukhari*, Vol. 1, 342

Companions of the Prophet

Most Muslim scholars define the companions (sahaba) of Prophet Muhammad to be the people who lived during his time period, and saw or heard him speak, even for a brief moment.

Islam teaches that no person should be praised or condemned without a valid reason regardless of their origin, belief, or color. According to the Noble Quran, those nearest to Allah are the ones who are the most pious, "Verily, the most honorable of you with Allah is that believer who has more piety and righteousness."[1] Neither blood relation, friendship, companionship, monetary status, nor social status play a role in nearness to Allah.

As for the companions (sahaba), the Noble Quran divides them into two groups. The first consists of those who were truthful and loyal, and had sacrificed their wealth and souls (i.e. life) to defend the cause of Islam. The Quran says, "Those who believed and emigrated and strove hard and fought in the cause of Allah with their wealth and their lives are far higher in degree with Allah. They are the successful. Their Lord gives them glad tidings of mercy from Him, that He is pleased (with them), and of Gardens for them wherein are everlasting delights. They will dwell therein forever. Verily, with Allah is a great reward."[2] Other numerous verses in the Noble Quran hail the good companions of the Prophet, such as the al-Badriyun, those who stood by the Prophet during the Battle of Badr, even though their number was less than one third of their enemies and their weapons were trivial compared to the weapons of their adversaries. They stood firm and sacrificed their lives and are among the best of examples for the Muslims.

---

[1] *Noble Quran, 49:13*
[2] *Noble Quran, 9:20-22*

Likewise, there were respected women among the *sahaba* who participated in the political, social, and economic life of Islam, such as Um Amarah who sacrificed four sons to defend Islam. While tending to the fatal injuries of one of her sons, Um Amarah herself went to the battlefield to fight the enemy. The Prophet witnessed her bravery and said about her, "O Um Amarah, who can bear what you are bearing?"

However, there is another group—the hypocrites, which the Noble Quran clearly describes. Numerous verses in the Noble Quran condemn their attempts to destroy the Muslim nation. In particular, there are two Surahs in the Noble Quran that refer to some of the companions as hypocrites: Surah 9 (*al-Tawbah* or The Repentance) and Surah 63 (*al-Munafiqeen* or The Hypocrites). In Surahtul Munafiqeen, the Noble Quran teaches that people should not be judged by their physical appearance, or even by their public actions, but rather by their sincerity and dedication to Allah, His Prophet, and the Muslim nation. This Surah says, "And when you look at them, their bodies please you, and when they speak, you listen to their words. They are as blocks of wood, propped up. They think that every cry is against them. They are the enemies. So beware of them; may Allah curse them. How are they denying the right path?"[3] These are the disobedient whom Allah will not forgive on the Day of Judgment, according to the Noble Quran, "It is equal for them whether you (Prophet Muhammad) ask forgiveness for them or do not ask forgiveness for them. Allah will not forgive them. Verily, Allah guides not the people who are rebellious, disobedient to Allah."[4] Although they performed the prayers and gave alms (*zakat*), these acts stemmed from their hypocrisy and desire to show off and were not for the sake of Allah. The Quran also says, "And nothing prevents their contributions from being accepted except that they disbelieved in Allah and in His Messenger and that they came to prayers only in a lazy state, and that they only offer

---

[3] *Noble Quran*, 63:4
[4] *Noble Quran*, 63:6

contributions (*zakat*) unwillingly."[5] Even when praying behind the Prophet himself, whenever a trade caravan would enter Madina, these hypocrites would leave their position in the prayer row to watch the caravan, rather than listen to the sermon of the Prophet of Allah. The Quran states, "And when they see some merchandise, or some amusement, they disperse headlong to it, and leave you (Muhammad) standing (while delivering the Friday *jum'ah* congregational religious sermon). Say: that which Allah has is better than any amusement or merchandise, and Allah is the best of providers."[6]

According to historical reports, some of these hypocrites who posed as the Prophet's "companions" were actually plotting to kill him.[7] The Noble Quran mentions that they had schemed to start a civil war in Madina:

> Verily, they had plotted sedition before and had upset matters for you—until the truth (victory) came, and the Decree of Allah became manifest though they hated it.[8]

> They (the hypocrites) say, 'If we return to Madina, indeed the more honorable (the chief of the hypocrites) will surely expel the abased (Allah's Messenger and his followers) from it .' But honor, power, and glory belong to Allah, His Messenger, and the believers, but the hypocrites know not.[9]

Some of these hypocrites established a masjid and invited the Prophet to inaugurate it, not to please Allah but to compete with the other Muslims and to cause disunity among the believers. Allah

---

[5] *Noble Quran,* 9:54
[6] *Noble Quran,* 62:11
[7] For further details see: *al-Waqidi, al-Maghazi,* Vol. 2, 989
[8] *Noble Quran,* 9:48
[9] *Noble Quran,* 63:8

ordered the Prophet to refuse their invitation and destroy that masjid which was based on hypocrisy:

> And as for those who put up a masjid by way of harming and disbelief, and to disunite the believers, and as an outpost for those who warned against Allah and His Messenger aforetime, they will indeed swear that their intention is nothing but good. Allah bears witness that they are certainly liars. Never stand therein. Verily, the masjid whose foundation was laid from the first day based on piety is more worthy for you to stand therein. In it are men who love to clean and purify themselves. And Allah loves those who make themselves clean and pure. Is he who laid the foundation of his building on piety to Allah and His good pleasure better, or he who laid the foundation of his building on an undetermined brink of a precipice ready to crumble down, so that it crumbles to pieces with him into the Fire of Hell? And Allah guides not the people who are the *dhalimun* (cruel, violent, proud, hypocrites, and wrongdoers). The building which they built will never cease to be a cause of hypocrisy and doubt in their hearts, unless their hearts are cut to pieces. And Allah is All-Knowing, All-Wise.[10]

Some of the hypocrites would approach the truthful Muslim believers and claim that they were genuinely part of the Muslim nation; yet, Allah informed the Muslims not to believe them, "They swear by Allah that they are truly of you while they are not of you, but they are a people (hypocrites) who intend to divide (the Muslim nation)."[11] The Muslim hypocrites, on countless occasions, insulted and offended the Prophet of Islam, the Quran says, "And among

---

[10] *Noble Quran,* 9:107-110
[11] *Noble Quran,* 9:56

them (the hypocrites) are men who hurt the Prophet and say, 'He is (lending his) ear (to every news).' Say, 'He listens to what is best for you, he believes in Allah, has faith in the believers, and is a mercy to those of you who believe.' But those who hurt Allah's Messenger will have a painful torment."[12]

Even the Prophet was unaware of some of the hypocrites in Madina. Although he knew of 'Abdullah ibn 'Ubay, the leader of the hypocrites, there were others in the Masjid of the Prophet—in the city of Madina—whom Allah did not inform him about. The Quran says, "And among the desert people (A'arab) around you, O believers, there are some hypocrites, and so are there some among the people of Madina. They exaggerate and persist in hypocrisy. Even you (Prophet Muhammad) know them not. We know them; We shall punish them twice and thereafter they shall be brought to a great, horrible torment."[13]

The acts of desecration to Islam and the Muslim society had reached such an extent by some of the hypocrites that Allah promised them eternal punishment. Therefore, Muslims should not extend the pleasure of Allah to all of the people around the Prophet without distinguishing between who was a true believer and who was a pretender. Nor should the Muslims refer to them as "the stars...whomever we follow, we will be guided." Imam al-Bukhari narrates:

> Allah's Messenger said, I will be there at the Fountain of Kawthar before you, and I will have to contend for some people, but I will have to yield. I will be saying, My Lord, they are my companions, they are my companions, and it will be said, You don't know what innovations they made after you.[14]

---

[12] *Noble Quran,* 9:61

[13] *Noble Quran,* 9:101

[14] *Sahih al-Bukhari,* "Book on Heart-Melting Traditions," Hadith 6089 and 6090, "Book on the Trials", Hadith 6527; *Sahih Muslim,* "Book on the

Imam al-Bukhari also narrates a similar version of this hadith:

Allah's Messenger said in the company of his companions, I will be at the Fountain waiting for those who will be coming to me from among you. By Allah, some people will be prevented from coming to me, and I will say, My Lord, they are my followers and the people of my *ummah* (nation). And He will say, You don't know what they did after you; they have been constantly turning back on their heels (from your religion).

Since many of the companions heard the Prophet saying this, a companion by the name of ibn Abu Mulaikah began then to include it in his supplication. It is reported that he used to say (in supplication), "O Allah, I seek refuge with You that we should turn back upon our heels or be put to any trial about our religion."[15]

Some Muslims claim that whoever disrespects any of the people around the Prophet is a not a Muslim or a believer. Certainly, criticizing a devout and genuine sahaba of the Prophet is completely forbidden and unacceptable. However, it should not be forgotten, that within the group of people around the Prophet there were some who were hypocrites, whom even the Prophet did not know of.[16] Nonetheless, Allah was well aware of them and even cursed those hypocrites who portrayed themselves as true companions of the Prophet, but in reality were not.

Scholars contend that to curse or speak ill about a companion is an abomination. However, within the Umayyad clan, there was a particular caliph who established a precedent for cursing a certain companion known for his devotion to Allah and Islam. If any Muslim

---

Virtues", Hadith 4250; Ibn Majah, "Book on Religious Rituals", Hadith 3048; *Musnad* Ahmad ibn Hanbal, Vol. 1, 384, 402, 406, 407, 425, 439, 453, and 455, Vol. 5, 387, 393, and 400

[15] *Sahih al-Bukhari*, "Book on Heart-Melting Traditions," Hadith 6104; *Sahih Muslim*, "Book on the Virtues," Hadith 4245

[16] *Noble Quran*, 9:101

who curses one of the companions is declared a disbeliever, then what would be the Islamic judgment regarding this caliph?

In addition, some hadiths claim that the companions were infallible, if they were infallible then why is it that after the death of the Prophet, some of the companions, from time to time not only disagreed with each other but their arguments even escalated into physical attacks. If they were infallible then why were they fighting each other? It has been documented that certain individuals from the companions of the Prophet were responsible for the assassination of the third caliph, 'Uthman ibn Affan. Should they still be regarded as equal to the pious companions of the Prophet?

If a hadith, such as "my companions are like stars...whomsoever you follow, you will be guided," indiscriminantly extends to all those companions who were around the Prophet, then such a hadith cannot be considerd authentic in the Shi'a school of thought since some of these same companions were reprimanded and cautioned about (to the Prophet) by Allah in the Quran.

Some of the companions commited sins without intending to defy Allah, and Allah promised them forgiveness, "And there are others who have acknowledged their sins. They have mixed a deed which was righteous with another that was evil. Allah shall turn to them in forgiveness. Surely Allah is Oft-Forgiving, Most Merciful."[17]

The Wives of the Prophet

Similarly, the wives of the Prophet are included in what was said about the companions of the Prophet, since blood relation or the bond of marriage alone does not ensure a safe passage to Paradise. Allah teachesus in the Noble Quran that only good deeds entitle the believers to success and to enter Paradise. Being a wife or a son or a daughter of the Prophet would not automatically grant success on the Day of Judgment, although it may grant them the fellowship of the Prophet and knowledge of his traditions.

---

[17] *Noble Quran*, 9:102

Almighty Allah puts forth in the Noble Quran a parable about the wives of two prominent messengers of Allah, Nuh and Lut, "Allah sets forth an example for those who disbelieve: the wife of Nuh and the wife of Lut. They were under two of our righteous slaves but they both betrayed (their husbands, by rejecting their doctrine), so they benefited them not against Allah, and it was said to them, 'Enter the Fire with those who enter it.'"[18]

Muslim historians narrate that some of the wives of the Prophet were not always on good terms with him. Imam al-Bukhari narrates from one of the wives of the Prophet, Lady 'A'ishah:

> The Apostle of Allah used to spend time with Zaynab bint Jahsh (one of his wives) and drink honey at her house. She (Lady 'A'ishah) further said, I and Hafsa (another wife) agreed that the one whom the Apostle of Allah visited first should say, I notice that you have an odor of "maghafir" (the gum of mimosa). He visited one of them and she told him this, whereupon he said, I have taken honey at the house of Zaynab bint Jahsh, and I will never do it again. After this, the following verse was revealed, referring to his abstention from honey, O Prophet! Why do you ban for yourself that which Allah has made lawful to you, seeking to please your wives (Lady 'A'ishah and Hafsa)? And Allah is Oft-Forgiving, Most Merciful.[19]

---

[18] *Noble Quran*, 66:10

[19] *Noble Quran*, 66:1; See *Sahih al-Bukhari*, "Book on the Interpretation of the Quran", Hadith 4531; *Sahih Muslim*, "Book on Divorce", Hadith 2694; al-Tirmidhi, "Book on Foods", Hadith 1574; al-Nisa'i, "Book on Divorce", Hadith 3367, "Oaths", "Vows", and "Crop Sharing", Hadith 3735, "Intimacy for Women", Hadith 3896; Abu Dawud, "Book on Drinks", Hadith 3227; Ibn Majah, "Book on Foods", Hadith 3314; *Musnad*, Ahmad ibn Hanbal, Vol. 6, 221; al-Darami, "Book on Foods" Hadith 18986

The Noble Quran also addresses Lady 'A'ishah and Hafsa exclusively, "If you two (wives of the Prophet) turn in repentance to Allah—but your hearts are so inclined (to oppose what the Prophet likes). But if you help one another against him, then verily Allah is his Protector—and Jibril, and the righteous among the believers, and the angels are also his helpers. It may be that if he divorced you, his Lord would give him, instead of you - wives better than you—Muslims submitting to Allah, believers, women obedient to Allah, who turn to Allah in repentance, worship Allah sincerely, given to fasting, or emigrants (for the cause of Allah)—previously married and virgins."[20]

These verses of the Noble Quran prove that not all the wives of the Prophet were the best of his companions.

For political, social, and economic reasons, as well as to spread the word of Allah, the Prophet had several wives and was patient with their mischief and rebellion (see Noble Quran, 66:4-5).

Historical Facts

Now, let us take an unbiased look at the history of Islam.

Imam Ali was the first male to embrace Islam.[21] He himself declared, "I started worshipping Allah nine years before anyone else in this nation started worshipping Him, except for Prophet Muhammad."[22]

The Prophet held two ceremonies of Brotherhood (mu'akhat) in which he made the Muslims brothers of each other. He did one before the migration to Madina and one afterwards.[23] In both

---

[20] Noble Quran, 66:4-5

[21] Ibn Abi al-Hadid al-Mu'tazili, Sharh Nahj al-Balaghah, Vol.13, 224

[22] al-Nisa'i, Khasa'is Amir al-Mu'minin, Vol. 13, 39 (Refer also to: Tarikh al-Tabari, Vol. 2, 316 and Vol. 5, 17 to see when other companions embraced Islam)

[23] al-Hakim, al-Mustadrak, Vol. 314; Fath al-Bari, Vol. 7, 211; Tarikh al-Khamis, Vol. 1, 353; al-Sirah al-Halabiyyah, Vol. 2, 220; al-Sirah al-Nabawiyyah, Ahmad Zayni Dahlan, Vol. 1, 155

Brotherhoods, the Prophet made brothers of himself and Imam Ali, Abu Bakr and 'Umar, 'Uthman ibn Affan and 'Abd al-Rahman ibn 'Auf, Hamzah ibn 'Abd al-Mutallib and Zayd ibn Haritha, Mus'ab ibn 'Umayr and Sa'd ibn Abi Waqqass, Salman al-Farsi and Abu Dharr al-Ghifari, and Talha and Zubayr.[24]

The Prophet ordered all of the gates which had access to the courtyard of the Masjid of the Prophet to be closed except the gate which connected to the house of Imam Ali, since the ritually impure (junub) were no longer allowed to enter the masjid before performing the ritual bathing (ghusl). However, the Prophet, Imam Ali, and Lady Fatima al-Zahra were exceptions to this rule, as an emphasis to the "Verse of Purity" (Noble Quran - 33:33). Even Hamzah, the uncle of the Prophet was saddened by this decision and came to the Prophet weeping. The Prophet told him, "I did not ban you, and I did not allow him (Ali); but it was Allah who allowed him."[25] Ibn Hanbal also narrates that many companions wondered about the Prophet's decision to exempt Imam Ali from having to shut his door to the masjid, the Prophet answered them by this sermon, "I commanded that these doors be closed except for the door of Ali. By Allah, it was not my own desire, but I was commanded by Allah, and I followed his command."[26] For this reason, the second caliph, 'Umar ibn al-Khattab, says, "Ibn Abi Talib has been given three virtues of which, if I had been given only one, it would have been better for me than everything in this life: the Messenger of Allah married him to his own daughter and she delivered offspring for him, the Prophet sealed all the gates to the

---

[24] Ibn Sa'ad, al-Tabaqat al-Kubra, Vol. 3, 102
[25] al-Isabah fi Ma'rifat al-Sahabah, Vol. 1, 373; al-Durr al-Manthur, Vol. 6, 122; al-Samhudi, Wafa' al-Wafa', Vol. 2, 477; al-Muttaqi al-Hindi, Kanz al-Ummal, Vol. 15, 155, and others
[26] Musnad Ahmad ibn Hanbal, Vol. 1, 175; Vol. 2, 26; Vol. 4, 369

Masjid of the Prophet except his door, and the Prophet gave him the banner on the Day of Khaybar."[27]

The Event of Thursday

Towards the end of the life of the Messenger of Allah, the Roman army was gathering on the border of the Islamic state, and the Prophet ordered all of his companions except for Imam Ali to leave Madina and to join the battalion of Usama ibn Zayd. Some of the prominent companions refused to join. The Prophet ordered them again to go, but they still refused. The third time, when they gathered in his house on a Thursday, four days before he passed away, the Prophet opened his eyes and saw that his companions had gathered around his deathbed. The Prophet asked for a pen and paper to write his will but one of the companions refused to give it to him, saying, "Verily, pain has overwhelmed him. The book of Allah is enough for us." Once the argument increased, the Prophet turned to them and said, "Go away from me. You should not argue in my presence."[28] 'Abdullah Ibn al-'Abbas says, "Disaster struck when they did not allow the Prophet to write his will."[29] Other historians narrate that on that day, the same companion said, "Leave him (the Prophet) alone. He is hallucinating."[30]

This situation occurred despite the clear command of the Noble Quran, "Obey Allah, and obey the Messenger that you may obtain mercy,"[31] and "He who obeys the Messenger has indeed obeyed Allah, but he who turns away, then we have not sent you (Muhammad) as a watcher over them."[32] This companion later on

---

[27] Ibn Hajar, *al-Sawa'iq al-Muhriqah*, Vol. 3, 9; al-Hakim, *al-Mustadrak*, Vol. 3, 125

[28] *Sahih al-Bukhari*, Vol. 4, 490, Hadith 1229; *Sahih Muslim*, Vol. 11, 89; Ibn Sa'ad, *al-Tabaqat al-Kubra*, Vol. 2, 36; *Misbah al-Munir*, Vol. 6, 34

[29] Shahristani, *al-Milal wal-Nihal*, Vol. 1, 22

[30] Sibt ibn al-Jawzi, *Tadhkirat al-Khawass*, Abu Hamid al-Ghazali, *Sirr al-'Alamin*, 21; *Tarikh* ibn al-Wardi, Vol. 1, 21

[31] *Noble Quran*, 4:80

[32] *Noble Quran* 3:132

confessed as to why he denied the Prophet's request during the "Event of Thursday," by saying that the Prophet had wanted to mention Imam Ali for leadership during his final days so he stopped him from doing that.[33]

Imam al-Bukhari reports on the authority of Sa'd ibn Jubayr from Ibn al-'Abbas:

> Thursday, and what about Thursday! Then he wept until his tears wetted the gravel. Thereupon I said, 'O Ibn al-'Abbas, what about Thursday?' He said, 'The Messenger of Allah said, Bring me (a pen and paper) so that I may write for you a document (by which following) you will never go astray.' But they disputed, while in the presence of the Prophet, there should be no disputing. They said, 'What is the matter with him?' Ask him. He said, 'Leave me alone. That which I suffer is better. I give you three wills: Drive the polytheists out of the Arabian Peninsula; grant delegations the same allowance that I used to give;' but he kept silent over the third, or he said it but I was made to forget it.[34]

The Suffering of Lady Fatima al-Zahra

One of the undeniable historical facts that all Muslim historians, regardless of their school of thought, unanimously agree upon is that the beloved daughter of the Prophet, Lady Fatima al-Zahra died approximately three months after him; as a result of the great pain and suffering she endured during the incident of the attack on her

---

[33] Ibn Abi al-Hadid al-Mu'tazili, *Sharh Nahj al-Balaghah*, Vol. 3, 114; Ibn Hajar, *Fath al-Bari 'ala Sahih al-Bukhari*, Vol. 8, 132

[34] *Sahih al-Bukhari*, "Book on Jihad and Marching," Hadith 2825; *Sahih Muslim*, "Book on the Bequest," Hadith 3089; Abu Dawud, "Book on Land Tax, Emirate, and Booty," Hadith 2634; *Musnad* Ahmad ibn Hanbal, Vol. 1, 222

house. She died at the age of 18 years and 7 months. On the day of her burial, Imam Ali addressed the Prophet at his grave and said:

> O Prophet of Allah! Peace be upon you from me and from your daughter who has come to you and who has hastened to meet you. O Prophet of Allah! My patience about your chosen daughter has been exhausted, and my power of endurance has weakened, except that I have ground for consolation in having endured the great hardship and heart-rending event of your separation. I laid you down in your grave when your last breath had passed, when your head was between my neck and chest. Verily, we are Allah's and verily, unto Him shall we return. Now the trust has been returned, and what has been given has been taken back. As to my grief, it knows no bounds, and as to my nights, they will remain sleepless until Allah chooses for me the house in which you are now residing. Certainly, your daughter will apprise you of the joining together of your people for oppressing her. You ask her in detail, and get all the news about the matter. This has happened when a long time had not elapsed, and your remembrance had not disappeared. My salaam be upon you both, and the salaam of a grief-stricken, not a disgusted or hateful person, for if I go away it is not because I am weary of you, and if I stay it is not due to lack of belief in what Allah has promised the ones who endure.[35]

Lady Fatima al-Zahra, three months after her father, the Messenger of Allah's death were all spent in grief and agony. She was never seen smiling, not even once after the death of her

---

[35] *Nahj al-Balaghah*, Sermon 202

father.[36] Her suffering increased day by day as a result of the injuries she sustained when one of the companions slammed the door on her, two days after her father's death, causing her to mis-carry her son, Muhsin. When Lady Fatima died, her husband Imam Ali buried her in the night. Only a handful of sincere companions participated in her funeral and he performed the prayers over her.[37]

She was also denied her inheritance from the Prophet Muhammad — mainly, a land outside Madina called Fadak—on the grounds that prophets do not leave inheritance. Imam Bukhari narrates that when Lady Fatima asked for her share of the Prophet's inheritance, she received the response that the Prophet had said, "We, the group of prophets, do not leave inheritance. What we leave is charity." Thus she was refused anything from her father's inheritance despite the fact that the Noble Quran gives examples of prophets inheriting from other prophets, such as, "And Sulayman inherited from Dawud."[38]

These incidents happened even though the Messenger of Allah had said, "Lady Fatima is a part of me. Whoever angers her, angers me."[39] Ibn Qutaybah records that Lady Fatima al-Zahra said to some of the companions, "I take Allah as a witness, and His angels, that you have angered me and did not please me, and when I meet with the Prophet, I will raise my grievances about you to him."[40]

Did the Prophet Order the First Caliph to Lead the Prayers Before his Death?

As mentioned earlier, the Prophet before his death ordered the majority of his companions to leave Madina and to join the battalion of Usama, in order to defend the Muslims against the Roman aggression. However, some of the companions refused his

---

[36] Ibn Sa'ad, *al-Tabaqat al-Kubra*, Vol. 2, 85
[37] *Sahih al-Bukhari*, Vol. 5, 177
[38] *Noble Quran*, 27:16
[39] *Sahih al- Bukhari*, Vol. 5, 35
[40] Ibn Qutaybah, *Al-Imamah wal-Siyasah*, Vol. 1, 14

commands and stayed in Madina, while Usama camped in an area called Jurf. Nonetheless, two people namely Lady 'A'ishah, the daughter of the first caliph and the wife of the Prophet and Anas ibn Malik, narrate that the first caliph led the prayers with the consent of the Prophet during his sickness, Lady 'A'ishah narrates, "The Prophet went to the masjid to lead the prayers while he was too weak to walk, and Abu Bakr was leading the prayers. The Prophet came and sat next to Abu Bakr who was leading the prayers."[41] However, this narration does not imply that the Prophet commanded the first caliph to lead the prayers since—despite his illness—he still went outside to lead the prayers. The other narrator, Anas ibn Malik is not considered as a unbiased source, according to the Shi'a school of thought.

Those historians who do relate that the first caliph was present in Madina during the time of the death of the Prophet, indicate that on the day the Prophet was destined to pass away at noon, Lady 'A'ishah ordered Bilal to tell her father that the Prophet wanted him to lead the morning prayers. Once the Prophet learned of this, he went out to lead the prayers himself, even though he was severly sick, leaning on Imam Ali and al-Fadl Ibn al-'Abbas. After removing the first caliph and leading the prayers, the Prophet then went back to his room in the masjid and said to Lady 'A'ishah, "You are as companions of Yusuf (Joseph)."[42]

This story has been narrated in various words by nine narrators: Lady 'A'ishah, 'Abdullah ibn Mas'ud, 'Abdullah Ibn al-'Abbas, 'Abdullah ibn 'Umar, 'Abdullah ibn Zam'a, Abu Musa al-Ash'ari, Buraydah al-Aslami, Anas ibn Malik, and Salim ibn Ubayd. However, an examination of these sources show that all the narrations go back to Lady 'A'ishah. In addition, there are also some unreliable individuals in the chains of narrators. Furthermore, even if the Prophet had appointed Abu Bakr to lead those prayers, this appointment would not imply an appointment to succeed the

---

[41] Ibn Kathir, *al-Bidayah wal-Nihayah*, Vol. 5, 253
[42] *Tarikh* al-Tabari, Vol. 2, 439; *Sirat* ibn Hisham, Vol. 4, 303

Prophet in all aspects of life, since during the Prophet's lifetime, he had permitted many people to perform the prayers, and of course, they are not considered as the caliphs;, such as Ibn Um Maktum who was blind.[43] Shaykh al-Islam Ibn Taymiyyah acknowledges that being a successor for certain tasks in life does not stretch to include succession after death. He adds that the Prophet had appointed many people, such as ibn Um Maktum, Bashir ibn 'Abd al-Mundhir, and others for certain tasks, such as leading the congregational prayers. Nevertheless, most of these people were not suitable for succession to the Prophet.[44]

In another slightly contrasting hadith, the famous historian and transmitter of hadith, al-Tabari[45] narrated that the first caliph, Abu Bakr was not in Madina at the time of the death of the Prophet, and when the Prophet was in extreme pain and could not go to the masjid to perform the prayers, Bilal, the *mu'adhdhin* (the caller to prayer) asked, "O Messenger of Allah! May my mother and father be your ransom, who will lead the prayers?"[46] The Prophet called upon Imam Ali. Then his wife, Lady 'A'ishah said to him, "We will call for you Abu Bakr," and his wife Lady Hafsa said, "We will call for you 'Umar." Thus, the Prophet's call did not reach Imam Ali, and the rest of the people came. Once they gathered around the Prophet, he said to them, "Go away. If I need you I will send for you." Then these companions left.[47]

The Ten who are Guaranteed Paradise

Tirmidhi narrates that the Prophet declared that ten of his companions were guaranteed paradise, while Imam al-Bukhari and Muslim (al-Dhahabi in his book, *Mizan al-I'tidal*) deny that the Prophet had ever made such a statement, as well as. This hadith counters logic on many levels, and as such, cannot be accepted. For

---

[43] *Sunan* Abi Dawud, Vol.1, 98
[44] Shaykh al-Islam Ibn Taymiyyah, *Minhaj al-Sunna*, Vol. 4, 91
[45] *Tarikh* al-Tabari, Vol. 2, 439
[46] *Musnad* Ahmad ibn Hanbal, Vol. 3, 202
[47] *Tarikh* al-Tabari, Vol. 2, 439

instance, Talha and Zubayr, who are both included in this hadith, ordered the killing of the third caliph 'Uthman—who is also included in this hadith. They are the same—Talha and Zubayr—who revolted against the legitimate caliph, Ali ibn Abi Talib after paying allegiance to him. Another individual included in this hadith is Sa'd ibn Abi Waqqass, who refused to pay allegiance to Imam Ali but did pay allegiance to Mu'awiyah. Another individual was 'Abd al-Rahman ibn 'Auf who revolted against the third caliph, 'Uthman ibn Affan and was killed by the Umayyads. The second caliph described ibn 'Auf as the "pharaoh of this nation."[48] The very notion that only ten of the Muslims should be guaranteed Paradise is illogical, since it exempts hundreds of other sincere and virtuous Muslims, such as Hamzah - *Sayyid al-shuhada* (Master of the Martyrs) and uncle of the Prophet, Ja'far ibn Abi Talib, Zayd ibn Haritha, Sa'd ibn Ma'adh, 'Ammar ibn Yassir, about whom the Prophet said, "He is filled with faith (*iman*) from head to toe," and Salman al-Farsi, about whom the Prophet said, "He is one of us, the *Ahlul Bayt*." Since the hadith of the ten who are guaranteed Paradise was narrated by Sa'id ibn Zayd, who was not on good terms with the Ahlul Bayt, the Shi'a school of thought can not accept it.

Abu Hurayra

The man who narrated the largest number of hadith—5,374 (446 of which are in Sahih al-Bukhari), although he says that he only spent three years with the Prophet[49]—was Abu Hurayra al-Dusi. He embraced Islam on the seventh year after the migration to Madina. Abu Hurayra himself says that only 'Abdullah ibn 'Umar narrated more traditions than he did, and that 'Abdullah used to write them down whereas he did not.[50] In fact, 'Abdullah ibn 'Umar only narrated 2,630 hadith, of which Imam al-Bukhari mentions only

---

[48] Ibn Qutaybah, *Al-Imamah wal-Siyasah*, 24

[49] Ibn Sa'ad, *Al-Tabaqat al-Kubra*, Vol. 4, 327; *Sahih al-Bukhari*, Vol. 4, 239; Mahmud Abu Riyyah, Shaykh al-Mudhirah Abu Hurayra. He proves that his companionship lasted one year and nine months.

[50] *Sahih al-Bukhari*, Kitab al-'Ilm, Vol. 1, 86

seven and Imam Muslim narrated, twenty. 'Umar ibn al-Khattab himself narrated only 527 hadith; while 'Uthman ibn Affan narrated 146; Abu Bakr, 142; 'A'ishah, the wife of the Prophet, 1,210; Jabir ibn 'Abdillah al-Ansari, 1,540; 'Abdullah ibn Mas'ud, 848; Abu Dharr al-Ghifari, 281; Um Salamah, the wife of the Prophet, 378; Ali ibn Abi Talib, 537; and Anas ibn Malik, 2,286.

Furthermore, Imam Muslim also narrates that the second caliph, 'Umar ibn al-Khattab beat Abu Hurayra on one occasion. [51] Abu Hurayra admits, "I have narrated to you several traditions that had I narrated them during the time of 'Umar, 'Umar would have lashed me with a stick."[52] It has been said that Abu Hurayra was the first narrator who was accused justly in Islam.[53] 'Umar al-Khattab said to him, "You have taken the money of the Muslims for yourself...."[54] 'Umar also told him once, "You have narrated too many hadiths, and most likely, you lie about the Prophet."[55] Ibn Hajar al-Asqalani says that the 'ulama unanimously agreed that lying about the Messenger of Allah is one of the cardinal sins (kaba'ir), and others went further to say, that whoever lies about the Prophet is an unbeliever (kafir). Al-Sam'ani states that narrations would not be accepted from someone who lied about the Prophet, even one time.[56]

Another example of the narrations of Abu Hurayra is found in the Sahih of Imam al-Bukhari. Abu Hurayra attributes the following advice to the Messenger of Allah, "When a fly falls into one of your goblets, immerse the entire fly inside the goblet and then take it out, and then consume the (contents of the) goblet, because on one wing of the fly is a disease, and on the other wing is the cure."[57]

---

[51] Muhammad al-Ghazzali, Fiqh al-Sirah, 41
[52] Ibid.
[53] Mustafa al-Rafi'i, The History of Arab Literature, Vol. 1, 278
[54] Ibn al-Athir, al-Bidayah wal-Nihayah, Vol. 8, 116
[55] Ibn Abi al-Hadid al-Mu'tazili, Sharh Nahj al-Balaghah, Vol. 1, 360
[56] al-Nawawi, al-Taqrib, 14
[57] Sahih al-Bukhari, Vol. 7, 22

Sahih Muslim narrates from Abu Hurayra that the Prophet slept until sunrise and missed the morning prayers![58] This hadith is not compatible with the Noble Quran which says, "Stand to pray all night, except a little—half of it, or a little less than that, or a little more—and recite the Quran in a slow style."[59] How could the Prophet, who never missed the midnight prayers, miss the obligatory morning prayers? Along the same line, in *Sahih Bukhari*, it narrates from Abu Hurayra that the Muslims were standing in their prayer rows about to pray, and that the Prophet had just finished the *Iqamah* when suddenly he remembered that he was junub (in a state of ritual impurity)![60] Al-Bukhari also narrates from Abu Hurayra that the Prophet said, "The *Shaytan* (Satan) confronted me and kept me busy!"[61] This hadith also diverges from the Noble Quran, which says, "When you want to recite the Quran, seek refuge with Allah from the Shaytan, the cursed. Verily, he has no power over those who believe and put their trust only in their Lord. His power is only over those who obey and follow him and those who join partners with him."[62]

Imam Muslim also narrates from Abu Hurayra that Lady 'A'ishah, the wife of the Prophet said:

> One day, the Messenger of Allah was lying in my house, revealing his thighs. Abu Bakr sought permission (to enter). He gave him permission, so he entered and spoke to the Prophet, and the Prophet remained in the same condition. Then 'Umar sought permission (to enter). He gave him permission, and he spoke to him while he was in the same condition. Then 'Uthman sought permission (to enter.) Once 'Uthman sought

---

[58] *Sahih Muslim*, Vol. 1, 310, 471
[59] *Noble Quran,* 73:2-3
[60] *Sahih al-Bukhari*, Vol. 1, 77
[61] *Sahih al-Bukhari*, Vol. 4, 151
[62] *Noble Quran,* 16:99

permission, he (the Prophet) sat down properly and covered himself. When he spoke to him and he left, I said, "You neither paid attention to Abu Bakr nor 'Umar, so why did you (when 'Uthman entered) cover your thighs?" The Prophet said, "Would I not be embarrassed in front of a man whom the angels are embarrassed in front of?"[63]

Ibn 'Arafa explains that most of such narrations were constructed during the time of the Umayyad Dynasty.[64] When Mu'awiyah reached power, he wrote to all his governors around the Islamic state, "For every virtue which is narrated by the Prophet on behalf of Imam Ali, I need a similar virtue to be said on behalf of the companions."[65]

Since hadiths are the second source of Islamic legislation all the contents and chains of narrators must be carefully examined and compared to the Book of Allah before being accepted. The Shi'a school of thought has strict criteria for judging the narrators of hadith and determining the authenticity any of ahadith.

---

[63] *Sahih Muslim*, Vol. 4, 1866, Hadith 2401

[64] Ahmad Amin, *Fajr al-Islam*, 213

[65] For further details, see: Ibn 'Abd al-Birr, *al-Isti'ab*, Vol. 1, 65; Ibn Hajar, *al-Isabah*, Vol. 1, 154; Ibn al-Athir, *al-Kamil fil-Tarikh*, Vol. 3, 162; *Tarikh al-Tabari*, Vol. 6, 77; *Tarikh ibn Asakir*, Vol. 3, 222; *Wafa' al-Wafa'*, Vol. 1, 31; *Tahdhib al-Tahdhib*, Vol. 1, 435; Ibn Abi al-Hadid al-Mu'tazili, *Sharh Nahj al-Balaghah*, Vol. 1, 116

Differences and Misunderstandings between the Shi'a and the Other Schools of Thought

'Abasa Watawalla (He Frowned and Turned Away)

This verse is one of the verses of the Noble Quran whose interpretation differs between the two main schools of thought. The majority of the Sunni scholars claim that the man who frowned and turned away from a blind person was the Prophet, while the Shi'a scholars say that the man who frowned and turned away was one of the companions of the Prophet; not the Prophet himself.

According to the Sunni scholars, the blind man was 'Abdullah ibn Um Maktoum. He is said to have come to the Prophet when the Prophet was conversing with a group of non-believers (Utbah ibn Rabi'ah, Abu Jahl ibn Hisham, al-'Abbas ibn 'Abd al-Mutallib, 'Ubay, and Umayyah ibn Khalaf) and was trying to incline their hearts towards Islam, since they were the leaders of Makkan society and if they embraced Islam then many others would follow them. The blind man came and interrupted the Prophet and asked him to teach him what Allah had taught him, not knowing that the Prophet was busy with this group of people. Thus according to the Sunni scholars the Prophet frowned.

The Shi'a interpretation of this verse, as narrated from the sixth imam of the Ahlul Bayt, Imam Ja'far al-Sadiq, is that the verse descended because one of the companions of the Prophet, who happened to be from Bani Umayyah, was sitting next to the Prophet and when the blind man came the man expressed a dislike and disgust at him, hence he turned his face away from him.[1] This

---

[1] *Tafsir Majma 'al-Bayan*, Vol. 10, 437 (in the narration of al-Sadiq)

interpretation is more in character with the Prophet since frowning was not one of the Prophet's characteristics, even with his enemies. Nor was it of the Prophet's character to be more inclined towards the rich and to abandon the poor. Allah attributes the highest moral character to the Prophet, "And verily you (Muhammad) are on an exalted standard of character."[2] "And by the mercy of Allah, you (Muhammad) dealt with them kindly. And had you been severe and harsh-hearted, they would have broken away from you."[3] "Verily, there has come unto you a messenger from among yourselves. It grieves him that you should receive any injury or difficulty. He is anxious for you to be rightly guided. For the believers, he is full of piety, kind and merciful."[4]

After all of these testimonies from Almighty Allah, it is difficult to believe that the Prophet would still frown and turn away from one of his blind companions, since he began and ended his mission by expressing his affectionate support to the needy, the blind, and the disabled in society, and spent nights without food to sympathize with the poor.

It is strange that some commentators would consider attributing this verse to one of the companions of the Prophet as an insult to the companions, but they would not consider the interpretation of this verse as an insult to the Prophet himself; even though he is the highest example of ethical and moral behavior, and is the master and leader of all the faithful.

The Father of Ibrahim and the Father of Imam Ali

According to Shi'a doctrine, all the messengers, prophets, and divinely ordained imams descended from monotheistic fathers, grandfathers, and ancestors. Allah states this when He addresses the Prophet Muhammad, "Who sees you, O Prophet Muhammad, when you stand up at night for prayers, and your movements among

---

[2] *Noble Quran*, 68:4
[3] *Noble Quran*, 3:159
[4] *Noble Quran*, 9:128

those who fall prostrating (among your ancestors)."[5] From this verse, we understand that the father, grandfather, and great-grandfathers of the Prophet—all the up to Adam—were believers in Allah; they did not associate anyone or anything with Allah.

Similarly, Prophet Ibrahim also descended from monotheists. According to history, his father died as a monotheist, thereafter, he became the custody of his uncle, who is metaphorically referred to as his "father" in the Quran.

Likewise, the father of Imam Ali, Abu Talib was also from a monotheistic descend. Logic dictates that such a man who fiercely defended the Prophet for many years and never yielded to the demand of the Quraysh to hand him over to them, and whose death, along with that of Khadijah, prompted the Prophet to call that year "the year of sadness" was a believer in Allah and one who died as a Muslim. Traditions found in some of the *sahhah,* saying that he is being punished by Allah should not be taken as authentic, and their chains of narrators must be doubted since politics played a great role in distorting the traditions of the Prophet; in addition to, the character assassination of great personalities of Islam, such as Imam Ali ibn Abi Talib.

Abu Talib's proper name was 'Abd al-Manaff or 'Imran. He defended the Prophet for forty-two years - before the Prophet started his mission and afterwards. It has been said about him, "Whoever reads the tradition of the Prophet will know that if it were not for Abu Talib, Islam would not continued its progress."[6] There is no doubt about the full submission and faithfulness of Abu Talib to the unity of Allah and the religion of Islam.

The Myth of the Distortion of the Noble Quran

Only one Quran exists, which was revealed by Almighty Allah to the Prophet Muhammad. No additions have been made to it nor

---

[5] *Noble Quran,* 2.218-219.
[6] Ibn Abi al-Hadid al-Mu'tazili, *Sharh Nahj al-Balaghah.* Vol. 1. 142.

have there been any deletions, and nothing in it has been rearranged or otherwise tampered with. Allah says, "We sent down the Book, and We are its protectors."[7] Unfortunately, some Muslims have the misconception that the followers of the Ahlul Bayt have a different Quran, yet if they were to visit the Shi'a Masajid, homes, or Islamic centers and meet with their individuals and scholars then they would discover that this accusation has no basis.

One of the prominent Shi'a narrators of hadith, Muhammad ibn 'Ali al-Qummi al-Saduq asserts, "Our belief is that the Quran which descended from Allah upon His Prophet is what we find today between the two covers, and that is what the people have in their hands—no more and no less than is, and whoever attributes to us that we say other than that, is a liar."[8] The Shi'a were always concerned over the correct transmission of the Noble Quran, and when the Prophet died, Imam Ali swore that he would not wear his robe except for prayers until he had gathered the entire Quran into one volume (mushaf).[9]

However, in some of the sahih books, some narrations assert that entire Surahs, even verses of the Noble Quran are missing or were lost. For example, Imam al-Bukhari narrates, "Verily, Allah sent Muhammad with the truth, and He sent down the Book upon him, and the verse of stoning was included in what was sent down to him. We recited it, retained it in our memory, and understood it. Allah's Messenger awarded the penalty of stoning to death (to the married adulterer and adulteress) and after him, we also awarded the penalty of stoning. I am afraid that, with the lapse of time, the people (may forget) and may say, 'We do not find the penalty of stoning in the Book of Allah,' and thus go astray by abandoning this duty prescribed by Allah. Stoning is a duty laid down in the Book of Allah for married men and women who commit adultery when

---

[7] *Noble Quran,* 15:9; For more details, see al-Mudhaffar, *Aqa'id al-Imamiyyah,* 41.

[8] *I'tiqadat* al-Suduq, 164

[9] al-Muttaqi al-Hindi, *Kanz al-Ummal,* Vol. 3, 127

proof is established, or if there is pregnancy or a confession."[10] Other narrations also erroneously indicate that there was a verse in the Noble Quran saying to stone the adulterers.[11]

Imam al-Bukhari also narrates from one of the companions that there was a verse in the Noble Quran stating that the abandoning of ancestors is *kufr* (disbelief);[12] but all Muslims know that no such verse in the Noble Quran exists. Some other narrations, from other sources suggest that many verses of the Noble Quran are missing. Lady 'A'ishah, for example, narrates that Surahtul Ahzab (33) used to have 200 verses during the time of the Prophet, but when the third caliph, 'Uthman ibn Affan compiled the Noble Quran, he could only find 73 of them.[13] 'Abdullah ibn 'Umar also narrates, "No one should say, 'I have taken (the judgment) from the entire Quran.' How does he know that this is the entire Quran? Verily, a great deal is missing from the Quran."[14] There are other claims as well which do not need to be mentioned further.

The intention here is not to pursue the issue of the false allegations of the distortion of the Noble Quran amongst the various schools of thought, since all the schools of thought should be respected. Yet, the point intended is that the Quran that the Shi'as follow is the same Quran that exists everywhere in the world, and there is no other hidden Quran, as some people claim.

---

[10] *Sahih al-Bukhari*, "Book on Penalties", Hadith 6327 and 6328, "Adherence to the Noble Quran and Sunnah", Hadith 6778; *Sahih Muslim*, "Book on Penalties", Hadith 3291; al-Tirmidhi, "Book on Penalties", Hadith 1351 and 1352; Abu Dawud, "Book on Penalties", Hadith 3835; ibn Majah, "Book on Penalties", Hadith 2543; *Musnad* Ahmad ibn Hanbal, Vol. 1, 23, 29, 36, 40, 43, 47, 50, and 55; Malik, "Book on Penalties", Hadith 1295 and 1297; al-Darami, "Book on Penalties" Hadith 2219

[11] "Book of the Virtue of the Quran", Vol. 6, 508 and Vol. 9, 212; *Sunan* Abu Dawud, "Book of Ahkam"

[12] *Sahih al-Bukhari*, "Kitab al-Fara'idh" Vol. 8, 540

[13] Suyuti, *al-Itqan fi Ulum al-Quran*, Vol. 1, 63

[14] Ibid., Vol. 3, 81

Mushaf Fatima

According to the narration of the Ahlul Bayt, when the Messenger of Allah passed away his daughter, Lady Fatima al-Zahra was in so much grief that Allah sent her an angel to console her, and that angel told her what would happen to her in the near future. She found comfort in this news, and her husband, Imam Ali recorded what the angel said. These writings were gathered in a book called *Mushaf Fatima*. Imam al-Sadiq says, "There is nothing unlawful or lawful in that book, but it says only what will happen in the future."[15] Other reports say that whenever the Messenger of Allah received a revelation, he would then explain it to his daughter, and she would write it in a book which was named *Mushaf Fatima*. The followers of the Ahlul Bayt believe that this book is now with the last Imam - al-Mahdi - of the school of Ahlul Bayt.

Mushaf Fatima is not a Quran or part of the Quran; and the only Quran that the followers of the Ahlul Bayt have and fully believe in is the one which was revealed to the Prophet Muhammad during his lifetime, which is available throughout the world.

Naming After the Prophets and the Imams

Some Muslim families who follow the school of Ahlul Bayt name their children after some of the prophets and imams in the manner of 'Abd al-Nabi, 'Abd al-Rasul, 'Abd al-Husayn, 'Abd al-Rida, and so on. Some people wonder whether this practice is permissible or not. Although the Prophet said that the best of names are those beginning with "'Abd" and "Muhammad," thus there is no harm in using the previous name because the name is not intended to be literal, and it does not imply that the specific child is a slave of the Prophet, Imam Husayn, or Imam Rida, or that the Prophet or the imams created him and are sustaining him. Rather, this sort of naming expresses gratitude, admiration, and love to those individuals such as the Prophet or the imams who dedicated their entire lives for the welfare of humanity.

---

[15] al-Kulayni, *al-Kafi*, Kitab al-Hujjah, 240

The Noble Quran itself uses the word "'abd" to mean other than the "servant of Allah" for example, the phrase *"min 'ibadikum"* (from your male slaves) does not mean that the slaves are worshipping their owner. The real slavery and ownership is for Allah, but allegorically, the name 'Abd al-Rasul implies that its bearer is a slave of Allah through the Prophet, since the Noble Quran states, "Whoever obeys the Messenger has obeyed Allah."[16] Again, the sense of slavery is to be taken allegorically and not literally.

Expressions like these find their way into a common speech in which people sometimes say the phrase "my master (*sayyidi*)," as a form of politeness. Some may even use the expression, "may I be your ransom (*ju'iltu fidak*)" without meaning it literally. In the Arabic language, these phrases express gratitude and thankfulness. Hence, by naming a person 'Abd al-Husayn or 'Abd al-Rida is in no way *shirk* (polytheism) to Almighty Allah, since all Muslims agree that He is the only One who deserves submission and obedience.

Visiting the Shrines of the Prophets and Imams

Touching or kissing the shrines of the Prophet and the imams does not imply shirk, nor does it associate that particular person with Allah, because Allah has the ultimate sovereignty in this universe, and Muslims submit to, worship, and seek help only from Him. Visiting the shrines is merely a gesture of respect. If the Prophet or the imams were alive then out of admiration people would shake their hands or kiss them. Since they are dead and people know that their shrines contain their sacred bodies, and perhaps their souls, then touching or kissing their shrines is a way of renewing allegiance and loyalty to these leaders. People are well aware of the fact that such shrines are made of ordinary material and the worshippers know that it has no power of benefit or harm; nevertheless, the respect and tribute is for what the shrines represent—the souls of these great personalities. Besides, being

---

[16] *Noble Quran,* 24.32.

present within the precincts of the sacred shrines gives the worshipper a sense of being in a sacred and holy place.

The Noble Quran teaches that when Prophet Yaqub cried over the separation of his son, Yusuf he lost his eye sight. Years later, Yusuf sent his shirt with one of his brothers and told him to put it on the face of his father so that he would regain his sight. The Quran says:

> Go with this shirt of mine and cast it over the face of my father. He will become seeing. And bring to me all your family. And when the caravan departed (Egypt), their father (who was in Palestine) said, "I do indeed sense the smell of Yusuf, if only you think me not sane." They (his family) said, "Certainly you are in your old error." Then when the bearer of glad tidings arrived, he cast it (the shirt of Yusuf) over his face, and he became seeing. He said, "Did I not say to you that I know from Allah that which you know not?"[17]

Although Yusuf's shirt was made of regular cotton material, which most of the people wore at that time, Allah made it bear His blessings because it touched the body of Yusuf. Thus with Allah's permission and authority, this shirt, when it was put on his face, enabled Yaqub to see.

If touching the shrine of the Prophet or Imam Ali or Imam Husayn is shirk (because these shrines are made from iron) then why do millions of Muslims touch the stones of the Holy Ka'bah? Were these stones brought from Paradise or were they ordinary stones used from the land of Hijaz? All Muslims agree that the Prophet kissed al-Hajar al-Aswad, the Black Stone on the Ka'bah, whereas he certainly did not go around kissing the stones in the alleyways and streets of Makkah, even though they may have been more alluring than the Black Stone. Today, in most countries, both

---

[17] Noble Quran, 12:93

Muslim and non-Muslim, the flag of a nation is so sacred that soldiers, even civilians kiss it and put it on their faces. Does that mean they are worshipping a piece of cloth? Certainly not! The moral behind these examples is that they are glorifying the ideas behind the stones or the shrines or the flags, and these are the principles and etiquette which were carried by the great leaders and countries.

Imam al-Bukhari narrates that whenever the Prophet did the ablution (*wudhu'*), the Muslims used to gather and collect the remaining water and pour it over their faces for blessings.[18] He also narrates that even the sweat of the Prophet was collected, in the following incident, "Um Salamah was putting some cloth under the Apostle of Allah when he slept. There was a lot of perspiration from his body. She brought a bottle and began to pour the sweat in that. When the Apostle of Allah woke up he said, 'Um Salamah, what is this?' She said, 'That is your sweat which we mix in our perfumes, and they become the most fragrant perfumes.'"[19]

"Sadaqa Allahu Al-Adheem" or "Sadaqa Allahu Al-Ali Al-Adheem"

There is practically no difference between saying, "*Sadaqa Allahu Al-Adheem*" (Allah the Most Great spoke the truth) or "*Sadaqa Allahu Al-Ali Al-Adheem*" (Allah the Most Great and Most High spoke the truth). This issue is perhaps the least significant between the schools of thought, especially since both sayings have been used occasionally in both, the Shi'a and the Sunni schools of thought.

However, the source of saying either of the above mentioned will be referred to the Noble Quran to dispel any misconceptions

---

[18] *Sahih al-Bukhari*, "Kitab al-Libas", Vol. 7, 199

[19] *Sahih al-Bukhari*, "Book on Taking Permission", Hadith 5809; *Sahih Muslim*, "Book on the Virtues", Hadith 4302; al-Nisa'i, "Book on Ornamentation", Hadith 5276; *Musnad* Ahmad ibn Hanbal, Vol. 3, 103, 136, 221, 226, 230, 231, and 287; Vol. 6, 376

which may arise in the minds of some Muslims who think that the word "*Al-Ali*" refers to Imam Ali ibn Abi Talib, though it does not.

The initial phrase "*sadaqa allah*" occurs in the Quran in many places such as, "Say: Allah has spoken the truth (*sadaqa Allah*)."[20] "*Al-Ali*" and "*Al-Adheem*" are among the 99 attributes of Allah. In the Noble Quran, Allah mentions His name coupled with "*al-Adheem*" by itself once,[21] and He mentions both attributes together twice (2:255 and 42:4) whereas "*Al-Ali*," which is mentioned in numerous verses, such as 22:62, 31:30, 34:23, 40:12, 4:34, 42:51, not to mention others. Therefore, mentioning both attributes together ("*Al-Ali*" and "*Al-Adheem*") is in no way a reference to the name of Imam Ali but rather imitating what the Noble Quran says in glorifying and exalting Almighty Allah.

Lamentation and Mourning the Tragedies of the Prophet and His Family

In general, the Noble Quran praises the act of crying and those who cry for a rightful cause. The Noble Quran describes many of the prophets and their followers by saying, "When the verses of the Most Gracious were recited unto them, they fell down prostrating and weeping."[22]

Similarly, it also describes certain believers as follows, "And they say, 'Glory be to our Lord. Truly, the promise of our Lord must be fulfilled,' and they fall down upon their faces weeping, and it adds to their humility."[23]

The prophet has been narrated to have cried over the deaths of several members of his family, such as his son Ibrahim, Imam al-Bukhari narrates:

---

[20] *Noble Quran* 3:95
[21] *Noble Quran* 69:33
[22] *Noble Quran,* 19:58
[23] *Noble Quran,* 17:109

The Messenger of Allah said, "A child was born unto me this night, and I named him after my father, Ibrahim." He then sent him to Um Sayf, the wife of the blacksmith, Abu Sayf. He (the Prophet) went to him, and I followed him until we reached Abu Sayf who was blowing fire with the help of bellows, and the house was filled with smoke. I hastened my step and went ahead of the Messenger of Allah and said, "Abu Sayf, stop it, as here comes the Messenger of Allah." He stopped, and the Apostle of Allah called for the child. He embraced him and said what Allah had desired. I saw that the boy breathed his last in the presence of the Messenger of Allah. The eyes of the Messenger of Allah shed tears, and he said, "Ibrahim, our eyes shed tears, and our hearts are filled with grief, but we do not say anything except that by which Allah is pleased. O Ibrahim, we grieve over you."[24]

The Prophet is also narrated to have wept for his uncle Hamzah:

When the Prophet returned from the Battle of Uhud and witnessed the women of Ansar weeping for their martyred husbands, he stood up and said, "But nobody is weeping for my uncle Hamzah," so the women understood that the Prophet desired people to weep for his uncle, and that is what they did. The crying for all the others ceased, except the crying for Hamzah.[25]

---

[24] Sahih al-Bukhari, "Book on Funerals", Hadith 1220; Sahih Muslim, "Book on the Virtues", Hadith 4279; Abu Dawud, "Book on Funerals", Hadith 2719; Musnad Ahmad ibn Hanbal. Vol. 3, 194

[25] Musnad Ahmad ibn Hanbal, Vol. 2

For his cousin Ja'far ibn Abi Talib[26] and his grandson Imam Husayn:

> Lady 'A'ishah narrates that when Husayn was a child, he came into the presence of the Prophet and sat on his lap, and Jibrail descended and told the Prophet that some of his nation would kill him (Husayn) and brought him a sample of the soil of Karbala, and said that the land was called al-Taff. When Jibrail left, the Prophet went out to his companions with the soil in his hand, and there were Abu Bakr, 'Umar, Ali, and Hudayfah while he was weeping. They asked him why he was weeping. He said, "Jibrail has informed me that my son Husayn will be killed in the land of al-Taff," and he brought me this soil from there and informed me that his final resting place will be there.[27]

Weeping for Imam Husayn is considered seeking nearness to Allah, because the tragedy of Imam Husayn is inextricably bound to the great sacrifice he endured for the sake of Allah. The Prophet, who knew the fate of his grandson, cried at his birth, cried when he was a child playing, and cried at his last moment before he died.

It is a natural act for people to show sympathy and affection towards those whom they love when they are stricken by grief and calamity. The Noble Quran says, "Say (O Muhammad): 'I do not ask any reward from you for this (preaching the message) but love for my relatives."[28] The Messenger of Allah explicitly told the Muslims

---

[26] *Sahih al-Bukhari*, Vol. 1, 152; *Sahih Muslim*, Vol. 1, Ch. "Weeping for the Dead", says, that the Prophet visited the grave of his mother, Aminah and cried and caused those around him to cry too. Ibn Abi al-Hadid al-Mu'tazili, *Sharh Nahj al-Balaghah*, Vol. 3, 387

[27] al-Mawardi al-Shafi'i, *A'lam al-Nubuwwah;* al-Muttaqi al-Hindi, *Kanz al-Ummal,* on the authority of Um Salamah (one of the wives of the Prophet).

[28] *Noble Quran,* 42:23

that this verse refers to his Ahlul Bayt—Ali, Lady Fatima, Hassan, and Husayn (for further information, see section on "Ahlul Bayt"). Thus, it is incumbent upon the Muslims to show love and sympathy for these individuals and the trials that they endured for the sake of Allah and to safeguard the religion of Islam.

None of the Ahlul Bayt died a natural death; all of them were either poisoned or killed by the sword in their struggle to defend Islam. None can fail to feel sorrow and pain for their tragedies. How can someone hear about the tragedy of 'Ashura, when Imam Husayn sacrificed 72 members of his family and companions for the sake of Allah, and was killed in such a tragic manner. The tragedy continued, when the women of his household—the family of the Messenger of Allah—were taken captive and dragged from city to city, accompanying the severed heads of Imam Husayn, his relatives and companions; how then can a person not cry? Even those who are not Muslim shed tears when hearing this story. If Muslims will cry over their own relatives, then how can they not cry over the family of the Prophet of Allah? Imam Husayn was not killed to be cried for; he gave his life to save the message of Islam and was martyred to fight tyranny and corruption. But the tears and sadness for Imam Husayn brings about a solemn pledge to follow in the footsteps of the Prophet and his family.

Showing sympathy about the tragedy of Imam Husayn and others from the Ahlul Bayt is neither an innovation nor is it a *bid'ah*. It must be noted that following the path of Imam Husayn is more important in the school of Ahlul Bayt, than merely crying for him.

Three Divorces in One Session

In Islam, divorce should be avoided as much as possible. The Prophet has been reported to have said that in the eyes of Allah, divorce is the most hated of all permissible acts; and it should only be performed as a last resort. Islam encourages family mediators to be called,[29] and divorce should be pronounced on three separate

---

[29] *Noble Quran,* 4.35.

occasions following a three-month waiting period before becoming irrevocable. The Quran says, "Divorce is only permissible twice, after which the parties should either stay together in a goodly manner, or separate with kindness. And if he has divorced her the third time, then she is not lawful unto him thereafter until she has married another husband. Then if the other husband divorces her, it is no sin on both of them that they reunite, provided that they will keep the limits ordained by Allah."[30]

Unfortunately, some non-Shi'a Muslim jurists allow a husband to divorce his wife irrevocably by issuing three divorce pronouncements in a single occasion, which is clearly opposed to the intent of the Noble Quran. It has been narrated in the books of *sahhah*, as well as in other books,[31] that the three divorce pronouncements in one session was considered as only one legal divorce during the time of the Prophet, the first caliph, and the first two years of the second caliph's rule. After that, the second caliph allowed the three pronouncements in one session to be considered as a three legal divorce, and hence the wife would be unable to go back to her husband.[32]

Khums in Islam

Khums is one of the pillars of Islam which was ordained by Allah and practiced during the life of the Messenger of Allah. *Khums* means "one-fifth," and indicates that one fifth of a person's excess income has to be dedicated, according to the Quran, for the following, "And know that whatever profit you make, verily, one-fifth of it is assigned to Allah and to the Messenger and to his family and also the orphans, the destitute, and the wayfarer, if you have

---

[30] *Noble Quran*, 2:229-230
[31] *Sirat* ibn Ishaq, Vol. 2, 191
[32] *Sahih Muslim*, "Chapter on the Three Divorces", Vol. 1, 575; *Musnad Ahmad* ibn Hanbal, Vol. 1, 314; al-Bayhaqi, Vol. 7, 336

believed in Allah, and in that which We sent down to our servant Muhammad."[33]

Khums, in brief, means paying one-fifth of the surplus of one's income after taking away the expenses of the person and his dependants. It consists of two equal parts: one being the share of the Imam, meaning that this part goes for constructing masjids, Islamic seminaries, Islamic schools, libraries, hospitals or clinics, orphanages, printing of the Noble Quran, hadith books, Islamic books and lectures, and others things which will benefit, defend, or propagate Islam. The second part is the portion for the poor *sayyids* (descendants of the Prophet), since they are banned from receiving *zakat* (charity).

Many historical references from different schools of thought mention that the khums existed during the time of the Prophet and was banned during the time of the first and second caliphs.[34] The interpretation by the Ahlul Bayt of the word "*ghanimtum*" in the Quran, chapter 8, verse 41 is "everything you gained"—whether from war, work, trade, or other sources, since Islam's history testifies that the Prophet took out one-fifth from the war booty, and also from assets other than the war booty during peacetime.[35] Other non-Shi'a scholars have supported this position.[36]

Temporary Marriage (Mut'ah)

Discussing the legality of temporary marriage should not in any way be perceived as encouraging youths to engage in such a practice. Permanent marriage is the norm which is recommended

---

[33] *Noble Quran,* 8:41

[34] *Sunan* al-Bayhaqi, Vol. 6, "Sahm Dhil Qurba"; *Musnad* al-Shafi'i, "al-Fay'", 187; *Sunan* Abu Dawud, Vol. 18, "al-Khums"; *Musnad* Ahmad ibn Hanbal, Vol. 1, 320; al-Muttaqi al-Hindi, *Kanz al-Ummal,* Vol. 2, 305; *Lisan al-Mizan,* Vol. 6, 148; Huliyat Abu Nu'aym, Vol. 2, 205; *Sahih Muslim,* Vol. 5, 198; *Sunan* al-Nisa'i, 177 and 178; *Tafsir* al-Tabari, Vol. 10, 5

[35] See for further details: *Musnad* Ahmad ibn Hanbal, Vol. 1, 314; *Sunan* ibn Majah, 839

[36] al-Qadi Abu Yusuf, *Kitab al-Kharaj,* 25-27

and encouraged in the Noble Quran and in the traditions of the Prophet and his Ahlul Bayt. Temporary marriage is the exception and should be used as a last resort whenever permanent marriage cannot be afforded or things become extremely difficult to bear (for one who can not get married). This section does not intend to discuss the advantages and disadvantages of such a marriage; but rather, to address its Islamic legality with respect to the Noble Quran and the traditions of the Prophet.

Marriage in Islam is a sacred institution, a commitment, and a pledge by two individuals to respect and uphold each other's will, dignity, honor, and aspirations. Marriage is of two types: permanent and temporary. Both share the same rules and restrictions and both need a prescribed form of proposal and acceptance, and marriage— even the permanent one—is open to conditions and restrictions. If the marriage is not confined to a period of time, then it would be considered as a permanent one, and if it is conditioned by a period of time, then it is a temporary one.

While disagreeing on the matter of temporary marriage, the scholars of other schools of thought agree that if a man intends to marry a lady for a short period of time without telling her that he will be divorcing her after a period of time and hides his intentions then the marriage is still valid. In such a case, temporary marriage seems more logical since the couple can actually agree on the terms and conditions beforehand with full honesty.

In essence, temporary marriage is a 'normal marriage' with a mutual agreement that is conditioned by a period of time. The conditions for this marriage include the following: a proposal and acceptance, a dowry for the woman, both parties have to consent and both have the freedom to accept or decline, both have to be sane, and a virgin woman must have her father's or guardian's approval. However, in temporary marriage, there is no obligation for sustenance or inheritance unless it is stated and conditioned in the marriage contract.

Regarding this practice, the Noble Quran says, "So with those whom you have engaged in *mut'ah* (temporary marriage), give them their dowries as prescribed."[37] In the tradition of the Prophet, scores of hadiths state the permissibility of temporary marriage. Imam al-Bukhari narrates, "There came to us the declarer of Allah's Messenger and said, 'Allah's Messenger has granted you permission to have temporary marriage,'—that is *mut'ah* with women."[38] He also narrates:

> We were on an expedition with Allah's Messenger and we had no women with us. We said, 'should we not have ourselves castrated?' He (the Prophet) forbade us to do so. He then granted us permission to contract temporary marriage for a stipulated period giving the women garments; and 'Abdullah then recited this verse, "O you who believe, do not make unlawful the good things that Allah has made lawful for you, and do not transgress. Allah does not like the transgressors."[39]

Imam al-Bukhari also narrates:

> "We went out with Allah's Messenger on the expedition to Banu al-Mustaliq. We were suffering from the absence of our wives, so we decided to have temporary marriage with women but by observing *'azl* (outside ejaculation). But we said, 'We are doing an act whereas Allah's Messenger is amongst us - why not ask him?' So we asked Allah's

---

[37] *Noble Quran*, 4:24

[38] *Sahih al-Bukhari*, "Book on Marriage", Hadith 4725; *Sahih Muslim*, "Book on Marriage", Hadith 2494; *Musnad* Ahmad ibn Hanbal, Vol. 4, 47, 51, and 55

[39] *Noble Quran*, 5:87; *Sahih al-Bukhari*, "Book on the Interpretation of the Noble Quran", Hadith 4249, "Marriage", Hadith 4683 and 4686; *Sahih Muslim*, "Book on Marriage", Hadith 2493; *Musnad* Ahmad ibn Hanbal, Vol. 1, 385, 390, 420, 432, and 450

Messenger and he said, 'It does not matter if you do not do it, for every soul that is to be born up to the Day of Resurrection will definitely be born (and nothing can prevent this from occurring).'"[40]

Imam Muslim also narrates instances of temporary marriage being done at the time of the Prophet[41] and gives clear reference that temporary marriage was lawful during the Prophet's time, the time of the first caliph Abu Bakr, and during part of the time of the second caliph—who was the one who prohibited it. Even after that time, it was still accepted by some Sunni scholars, such as al-Qurtubi who considered it as a lawful form of marriage and that it had been agreed upon by the predecessors and the successors (the *salaf* and the *khalaf*).[42]

The leaders of the Ahlul Bayt argue that according to the Noble Quran no one has the authority to make any act lawful or unlawful by his own desire. If there were an interest in banning temporary marriage then Allah, the All-Knowing would have done so through His Prophet.

Mut'at al-Hajj

Mut'at al-Hajj means that Muslims are free from the restrictions of *ihram* (ritual consecration) during the time between *'umrah* and the *hajj*, as the Noble Quran states in 2:196 – "Complete the hajj and the 'umrah for God's sake, and if you are prevented, then [make] such [sacrificial] offering as is feasible. And do not shave your heads until the offering reaches its [assigned] place. But should any of you be

---

[40] *Sahih al-Bukhari*, "Book on Types of Selling", Hadith 2077, "Setting Free", Hadith 2356; *Sahih Muslim*, "Book on Marriage", Hadith 2599; al-Tirmidhi, "Book on Marriage", Hadith 1057; al-Nisa'i, "Book on Marriage", Hadith 3275; Abu Dawud, "Book on Marriage", Hadith 1855-1857; Ibn Majah, "Book on Marriage", Hadith 1916; *Musnad* Ahmad ibn Hanbal, Vol. 3, 88; Malik, "Book on Divorce", Hadith 1090, al-Darami, "Book on Marriage", Hadith 2126 and 2127

[41] *Sahih Muslim*, "Book of Marriage", Ch. 3, Narrations 15-17

[42] *Tafsir* al-Qurtubi, Vol. 5, 132; *Tafsir* al-Tabari

sick, or have a hurt in his head, let the atonement be by fasting, or charity, or sacrifice. And when you have security—for those who enjoy [release from the restrictions] by virtue of the 'umrah until the hajj—let the offering be such as is feasible. As for someone who cannot afford [the offering], let him fast three days during the hajj and seven when you return; that is [a period of] complete ten [days]. That is for someone whose family does not dwell by the Holy Mosque. And be wary of God, and know that God is severe in retribution."

However, spousal relations between the time of 'umrah and hajj were prohibited by the second caliph, 'Umar ibn al-Khattab who declared, "O people, three things existed during the time of the Messenger of Allah that I prohibit and make unlawful and will punish for: Mut'ah al-Hajj, mut'ah al-nisa (temporary marriage), and 'hayya 'ala khayr al-'amal' (in the adhan)."[43] Similarly, he also said, "Two types of mut'ah existed during the time of the Messenger of Allah, and I prohibit them and will punish for them: mut'ah al-hajj and mut'ah al-nisa."[44]

Suyuti reports that 'Umar ibn al-Khattab was the first to introduce the tarawih prayers, lashed eighty lashes (instead of one hundred) as a punishment for drinking, prohibited mut'ah marriage, performed four takbirs (instead of five) in the funeral prayers, and many other things.[45]

Tirmidhi narrates that 'Abdullah ibn 'Umar was asked about mut'at al-hajj. He said that it is lawful. The person pointed out that 'Abdullah's father had been the one to prohibit it. 'Abdullah ibn 'Umar answered, "If my father prohibited that, and the Messenger

---

[43] *Sharh al-Tajrid,* Musnad Ahmad ibn Hanbal, Vol. 1, 49

[44] *Tafsir* Fakhr al-Razi, Vol. 2, 167; *Sunan* al-Bayhaqi, Vol. 7, 206; *Bidayat al-Mujtahid,* Vol. 1, 346; *Al-Muhalla,* Vol. 7, 107; al-Jassas, *Ahkam al-Quran,* Vol. 1, 279; *Tafsir* al-Qurtubi, Vol. 2, 370; *al-Mughni,* Vol. 7, 527; *al-Durr al-Manthur,* Vol. 2, 141; *Kanz al-'Ummal,* Vol. 8, 293; *Wafayat al-A'yan,* Vol. 5, 197

[45] al-Suyuti, *Tarikh al-Khulafa',* 137

of Allah did it, which one do we have to follow—my father or the commands of the Messenger of Allah?"[46]

---

[46] *Sahih* Tirmidhi, Vol. 4, 38

Conclusion

A Call for Muslim Unity

Discussing historical facts or jurisprudential differences should not in any way discourage Muslim unity, since the majority of Muslim historians from all schools of thought agree on similar historical facts. Differences between the philosophers, scholars and thinkers of the schools of thought can be either constructive or destructive. If they lead to the fragmentation of the Muslim nation, then they are unacceptable, as the Noble Quran says, "But they have broken their religion among them into sects, each group rejoicing in its belief."[1] Such groups of people support ideas which are not based on the truth and use them only to serve their own purposes, whereas the Noble Quran refers all arguments to one source, "And obey Allah and His Messenger, and do not dispute with one another lest you lose courage, and your strength depart, and be patient; surely, Allah is with those who are patient."[2] Unfortunately, the weakness of the Muslim world today is because of this type of disunity.

Nonetheless, constructive differences is a sign of a healthy society in which people compete for what is best, "If Allah willed, He would have made you one nation (religion) but that He may test you in what He has given you. So strive (as in a race) in good deeds."[3] Differences in scientific and jurisprudential opinions can lead to progress and prosperity, and on a philosophical level, they are beneficial if they lead to certainty (*yaqeen*), since all people must doubt, question, and differ from a matter before arriving at the truth. Therefore, Islam does not reject reasoning in the field of

---

[1] *Noble Quran*, 23:53
[2] *Noble Quran*, 8:46
[3] *Noble Quran*, 5:48

jurisprudence (*ijtihad*), as long as it is not contaminated with politics or personal aims and conceit. Thus all Muslim scholars agree that *mujtahid* (juristic scholar) receives two rewards for every correct decision, and at least one for every incorrect one because he is endeavoring with all of his effort to reach the correct decision.

Nevertheless, Muslim unity is one of the goals of Muslim society and is an obligation upon all Muslims, both individually and collectively. Allah says in the Noble Quran, "Truly, your nation is one united nation, and I am your Lord,"[4] and "Verily this (your nation) is one nation, and I am your Lord, so uphold your duty to Me."[5] Throughout the twenty-three years of his propagation, the Messenger of Allah emphasized the unity of his nation and called them "My Nation (*Ummati*)." The Noble Quran gives six meanings for the word ummah: a group of people, an example, adherence to a religion, a religion itself, the time, and a group that follows one tradition and one way. However, it is not used for a group that does not follow one tradition and one way.

The concept of unity itself is discussed in the Noble Quran on three levels. Foremost, it is the unity of humanity, "O mankind! We have created you from a male and a female, and made you into nations and tribes that you may know one another. Verily, the most honorable of you with Allah is the one who has piety."[6] The aim of this unity is to direct all the racial, tribal, and religious differences into a constructive direction. Thus the emphasis on "knowing one another" (*li-ta'arifu*) is that people should find mutual understanding rather than conflict, so that no one is denied the rights for life and prosperity.

The second form is within the unity of the People of the Book (or the monotheistic religions), for which the Quran says, "Say (O Prophet Muhammad): O People of the Book! Come to a word that is just between us and you, that we worship none but Allah, and that

---

[4] *Noble Quran*, 21:92
[5] *Noble Quran*, 23:52
[6] *Noble Quran*, 49:13

we associate no partners with Him, and that none of us will take others as lords besides Allah. Then if they turn away, say: Bear witness that we are Muslims."[7] The Noble Quran reiterates that the People of the Book were asked to worship only Allah, "And they were commanded not, except that they should worship Allah and worship none but Him alone."[8] The essential monotheistic unity of the People of the Book exists, but it should not be taken to mean that there are no differences between their rules and laws and that of Islam's. While the original way (din/religion) is seen throughout all monotheistic religions, the practical implementation—i.e. the law—is different according to the Quran, "To each among you We have prescribed a law, and a clear way. If Allah willed, He would have made you one nation but [His purposes require] that He test you in respect to what He has given you."[9]

Of course, the third unity that the Noble Quran speaks of is the unity of the Muslim nation, "And hold fast, all of you together, to the rope of Allah, and be not divided among yourselves."[10] Muslim unity has two fundamental purposes - one is to uphold the Noble Quran as the constitution of life, and second, is to accept our mutual responsibility towards each other as Muslims, for the Messenger of Allah has said, "Whoever does not care about the affairs of the Muslims is not one of them," and "Whoever hears a man calling 'O Muslims!' and does not respond is not a Muslim." He also used the parable of the human body to describe the Muslim nation - if one part suffers, the entire body will suffer. One of the greatest achievements of the Messenger of Allah was to unite hundreds of fragmented tribes throughout the Arabian Peninsula into a single strong nation. When he united them, he did not eliminate differences of opinion between them, but rather, he enabled them to have dialogue with each other and to come to a sense of mutual understanding. Under this philosophy, the Muslim nation was a

---

[7] *Noble Quran, 3:64*
[8] *Noble Quran, 98:5*
[9] *Noble Quran, 5:48*
[10] *Noble Quran, 3:103*

powerful nation in the past, and only with this understanding it would be able to return to this respected position among the nations of the Muslim world and have the same significant role that it did in the past.

A modern example that the Muslim countries should examine is the European Union in which several states of different languages, cultures, ethnicities, religions, and political agendas have unified under one monetary system, economic agenda, and political front. The Muslim governments could be similarly united if they so chose. The first step to such a unity is to increase the regular conferences and seminars which are held by Muslim intellectuals and scholars and aim to bridge the gap between the schools of thought.

In short, differences of opinion, when properly channelled, are an asset to the intellectual growth of the Muslim nation and are a sign of the vitality of the Islamic culture. The competition arising between different scholars, from all schools of thought, should encourage them to strive with their maximum effort to reach the best decisions, and ultimately, the truth. Diversity should not lead to division and fragmentation; on the contrary, it is part of the unity, just as it was in the society created by the Messenger of Allah 1,400 years ago. We would like to encourage all the scholars and intellectuals of Islam to continue the discussions on the juristic and philosophical issues under the umbrella of *la ilaha illa Allah Muhammadar rasul Allah (There is no entity worthy of worship except for Allah and Muhammad is the Messenger of Allah)*, and with the spirit of brotherhood and faith. And ultimately, we ask Allah, the Almighty for His guidance and wisdom.

> O you who believe! Fear Allah as He should be feared, and die not except in a state of Islam (submission to Allah). And hold fast—all of you together—to the rope of Allah, and be not divided among yourselves, and remember Allah's favor on you, for you were enemies, one unto another, but He joined your hearts together so that by His grace

you became brethren. And you were on the brink of a pit of fire, and He saved you from it. Thus Allah makes His signs clear to you, that you may be guided. Let there arise out of you a group of people inviting to all that is good, enjoining the good and forbidding the evil, and it is they who are the successful. And be not as those who divided and differed among themselves after the clear proofs had come to them. It is they for whom there is an awful torment on the Day when some faces will become white, and some faces will become dark. As for those whose faces will become dark (to them it will be said), "Did you reject faith after accepting it? Then taste the torment for rejecting faith." And as for those whose faces will become white, they will be in Allah's mercy. Therein they shall dwell forever. These are the verses of Allah. We recite them to you in truth, and Allah wills no injustice to mankind.[11]

صدق الله العلى العظيم

---

[11] *Noble Quran*, 3.102:108

References

The Noble Quran
'Abqariyat 'Umar
Al-Bidayah wal-Nihayah
Al-Durr al-Manthur
Al-Istibsar
Al-Isaba fi Tamyiz al-Sahaba
Al-Kafi
Al-Milal wal-Nihal
Al-Mustadrak 'ala Sahihayn
Al-Saqifah
Al-Sawa'iq al-Muhriqa
Al-Tabaqat al-Kubra
Al-Tahdhib
Asbab al-Nuzul (al-Wahidi)
Kanz al-'Ummal
Khasa'is al-Nisa'i
Lisan al-Mizan
Ma'alim al-Madrasatayn
Man La Yahduruhu Faqih
Musnad of Ahmad ibne Hanbal
Nadhariyyat al-Khalifatayn
Nahjal-Balaghah
Sahih al-Bukhari
Sahih Muslim
Sahih al-Tirmidhi
Sharh Nahjal-Balaghah
Sirat ibn Hisham
Sunan Abu Dawud
Sunan Ahmad Muwatta' Malik
Sunan al-Bayhaqi
Sunan al-Darqatni
Sunan al-Darimi
Sunan al-Nisa'i
Sunan ibn Majah
Tafsir al-Fakhr al-Razi

Tafsir al-Hasakani
Tafsir al-Kashshaf
Tafsir al-Qurtubi
Tafsir Ruh al-Ma'ani
Tafsir al-Tabari
Tafsir al-Tha'labi
Tadhkirat al-Khawas
Tarikh ibn Asakir
Tarikh ibn al-Athir
Tarikh Baghdad
Tarikh al-Aqd al-Farid
Tarikh ibn Kathir
Tarikh al-Khulafa'
Tarikh al-Tabari
Usd al-Ghabah
Yanabi' al-Muwadda

Glossary

A

Adhan: Call to prayer.

Ahlul Bayt: Designated family members of the Prophet Muhammad.

Ahl al-sunnah wal-jama'ah: Sunni tradition.

al-Kaba'ir: Cardinal sin.

Alawiyiin: The descendants of Imam Ali.

Amanah: Trust.

Amr: Command.

'Asr: Muslim afternoon prayer.

Awliya': (Plural of *wali*): leader, guardian, friend, master, slave, etc.

Azl: Outside ejaculation.

B

Bay'ah: Paying allegiance.

D

Dhalimeen (also spelled: dhalimun and dhalamu): Cruel, violent, proud, hypocrites, or wrongdoers.

Dhuhr: Muslim Noon Prayer.

Dhul Hijjah: The twelfth month of the Islamic calendar.

Dhulm: Oppression.

Du'a: Supplication.

E

Eid: Muslim holiday.

F

Faltah: Mistake.

Fajr: Muslim Dawn prayer.

Fatawa: A religious decision.

Fiqh: Islamic jurisprudence.

Fitna: Dispute, also trial or test.

G

Ghusl: Ritual bathing.

H

Hadith: Actions, words, and consents of the Prophet in matters pertaining to the meaning and practices of Islam which have been transmitted through a line of narrators.

Hijaz: Arabian Peninsula.

Hijrah: Immigration of the Prophet Muhammad from Mecca to Madina.

Hujjah: Proof.

Hukm: Decision.

I

Ibn (ibn): Son of...

Ihram: Ritual consecration.

Imamiyyah (Imami or Imamah): Succession to the Prophet.

Imams: Leaders after the Prophet (i.e. the 12 Imams).

Iman: Faith.

Ijtihad: Jurisprudence.

Iqaama: The call that signals the beginning of the prayer.

Isha: Muslim Night prayer.

J

Jama'ah: A group.

Jihad: Struggle. There are two types of struggles in Islam – the Greater Struggle (*jihad al-akbar*) which is the fighting against ill-desires of the self and the Lesser Struggle (*jihad al-asghar*) defending Islam in the warfront.

Junub: Being in a state of ritually impurity.

K

Kaffarah: Penalty money.

Kafir: Disbeliever.

Khilafa: Successorship or leadership.

Khumra: A solid piece of dirt or a piece of straw.

Khums: A form of charity described as: one-fifth of the surplus of one's income after taking away all legitimate expenses for a the person and his dependants.

M

Madhahib (madhhab): Schools of Islamic thought.

Maghafir: The gum of mimosa.

Mawla: Leader.

Miskeen: Destitute.

Mu'adhdhin: A person who makes the call to prayer.

Mu'akhat: Brotherhood.

Mubahilah: Malediction.

Muhkam: Fundamental or basic.

Mujtahid: A juristic scholar.

Mushaf: A book or volume.

Mushrik: One who associates something or someone with Allah.

Mustahhab: Recommended.

Mut'ah: Temporary marriage.

Mutashabah: Allegorical.

Mut'ah al-Hajj: Means that Muslims are free from the restrictions of *ihram* during the time between *'umrah* and the *hajj.*

Muwaddah: Affection.

N

Nawafil: Recommended Muslim prayers.

Nifaq: Hypocrisy.

Q

Qa'im: Firmly established.

R

Ruku: Bowing down.

S

Sabr: Patience.

Sadaqa: General charity.

Sahaba: Companions of the Prophet.

Sha'ban: The 8th month of the Muslim calendar.

Sahih: Authentic.

Salaf: Predecessors.

Salat: Prayer.

Salat al-Layl: The recommended, night Muslim prayer.

Sayyid: Master. Also means and elder or a descendent of the Prophet Muhammad.

Shaytan:Satan.

Shirk: Polytheism.

Shura: Consultation.

Sirat: Path.

T

Tabi'in: The following generation after the Prophet.

Taharah: Purity.

Takbir (takbirs or takbirats): Saying "Allah Akbar" which means 'Allah is Greater than everything else'.

Tarawih Prayer: Special prayers offered during the nights of Ramadan.

Tashhahud: Testimony.

Thaqalayn: A hadith of the Two Weighty Things [the Noble Quran and the Ahlul Bayt].

U

Ummah: Muslim nation.

Usul: Foundations.

W

Wali: Guardian.

Warith: Inheritor.

Wazir: Minister.

Wilat: Rulers.

Wudhu: Ablution.

Y

Yaqeen: Certainty.

Z

Zakat: Alms-giving.